Dinner on
the Grounds

THE ULTIMATE CHURCH COOKBOOK
BY
DARRELL HUCKABY
AND A HOST OF HEAVENLY COOKS

Published by
Southland Press
1108 Monticello St.
Covington GA 30014

1st Edition
1st Printing--1999
2nd Printing--2003

Cover Design by The Adsmith, Inc.
Athens, Georgia

Our cover photograph depicts a 1951 church dinner at
Port Wentworth United Methodist Church near Savannah.
submitted by
Arnease Moore, Rincon, GA
Window Drawing by Susan Edwards

ISBN   0-9647867-7-X

For Mama

AUTHOR'S NOTE

The idea for this book came to me in the summer of 1996 when, on behalf of St. Simons Press, I was working on a cookbook for the Blue Willow Inn in Social Circle, GA. It took three years for the project to come to fruition, but those involved believed that it was worth the wait.

My lovely wife, Lisa, was my partner in this project. We solicited recipes and stories from ministers and congregations across North and South Georgia. There was a great interest in our project and we received support from across the state of Georgia and beyond. Although most of the churchs we contacted were Methodist, we also received contributions from good cooks from a variety of denominations.

This book was originally released in December of 1999. Dedicated to my mother, Tommie Huckaby, she was able to see the very first copy, which arrived a week before her death.

I hope the reading of this book carries you back to a simpler time, as the writing and compiling of the book has brought back so many precious memories to me.

To those who contributed to this book I offer a special thanks. Words can not express the gratitude due to my mother-in-law, Bitzi Potts, for the typing and retyping she did. To Lisa, the wonderful life partner God has given me, I express my eternal love and thanks.

And thanks to my partners at Southland Press for once again making this book, which has been out of print for almost two years, available to the public.

Once again, dinner's finally ready.

Come and get it!

TABLE OF CONTENTS

ABOUT THE AUTHOR

Darrell Huckaby is a husband, father, teacher, coach, and author. Raised in the north Georgia mill village of Porterdale, he attended Newton County High School in Covington and graduated from the University of Georgia with a BSED in 1975. He returned to graduate school at UGA and received his MSED in 1995.

He was "raised" in the Julia A. Porter United Methodist Church in Porterdale. Darrell is married to the former Lisa Potts of Conyers. They live on her family farm in Rockdale County and have three children; Jamie, Jackson Lee, and Jenna. Lisa is a nurse-midwife and practices in Rockdale County. The Huckabys are members of Rockdale Baptist Church in Conyers.

Darrell Huckaby is a columnist for the Citizen Newspapers in Conyers and Georgia Goodlife Magazine. His first book was a novel, *Need Two*, which was published in 1995. Huckaby was nominated as Best New Georgia Author for his work which recounts the misadventures of two college students on a road trip to New Orleans to watch Georgia play Notre Dame in the Sugar Bowl. The author insists the story is not biographical, but few believe him. His other books are *Grits is Groceries, Southern Is as Southern Does*, and *Hard Rock to Solid Rock*, the true story of the dramatic conversion of former rock musician and current United Methodist minister, Lenny Stadler.

In his leisure time Huckaby follows sports, especially UGA football and travels with his family. He also enjoys public speaking and talks to a large number of churches and civic groups each year.

PRECIOUS MEMORIES—HOW THEY DO LINGER

Honesty compels me to admit that as a young child, church sometimes seemed to drag along for me. I was fine during the early part—the opening hymn, the Gloria Patria, the Apostle's Creed—even the anthem. But somewhere along about the morning prayer I would begin to get a little antsy. My collar would tighten, my shoes would feel uncomfortable, and my clothes would invariably begin to make me itch. At no time were these discomforts more evident than those special days—homecoming, fifth Sunday, or days when we'd welcome a new preacher—when the ladies (and men) of Julia A. Porter Methodist Church in Porterdale, Georgia would celebrate the special occasion with dinner on the grounds, following the morning services.

Dinner on the grounds! What precious memories those words bring back. Memories of a slower, simpler lifestyle. Memories of a time when there were no McDonalds or Wendy's or Captain D's, and the closest Chinese restaurant could have been in Shang Hai for all I knew of such matters. The smells that came through the open window of our little mill village church could tempt a Bishop. We always drew extra large crowds on days that dinner on the grounds would be served, and no Methodist preacher worth the water he used to sprinkle with could resist the opportunity to preach an extremely eloquent (translation—long) sermon when a large crowd was gathered.

Of course, that made the wait almost intolerable, but the meal was always worth the wait. So much good food! Casseroles, made from scratch; fried chicken and roast beef and ham; pickles and relish of every description; every garden fresh vegetable known to man; huge wash tubs of sweet ice tea and lemonade; a black kettle of Brunswick stew, slow cooked all night over an open fire; desserts galore--cakes, pies, cookies, brownies--the list is endless and the memories are precious.

I hope this book will help preserve those memories

Darrell Huckaby

7

CASSEROLES

"But he said to his disciples,
'Have them sit down
in groups of about fifty each.'
The disciples did so and everybody sat
down. Taking the five loaves and the two
fish and looking up to heaven,
he gave thanks and broke them.
Then he gave them to the disciples
to set before the people. They all ate
and were satisfied . . ."

Luke 9: 14-17

CHAPTER ONE

Examine the scripture on the previous page. The first dinner on the grounds in the history of Christ's church! Well, it might have been, anyway. What we do know is that Jesus knew the importance of food and fellowship. His disciples had come to him, begging the Master to allow them to send the folk home who had come to hear him. I'm sure Jesus was part Methodist. He had a great crowd to preach to and wasn't about to lose them. Send folks home and they might not come back!

He instructed Simon Peter and the boys to gather up what they could find and make do. God is pretty wonderful at making something out of nothing. They found a little ol' boy whose mama had packed him a lunch. They asked the young man to share, and he was happy to do so. Isn't that what a church dinner, particularly a dinner on the grounds, is all about? Didn't they get started so we could stay and revel in the presence of Christ's spirit and share what we had with one another?

What Dr. Luke didn't tell us in his scripture was how the disciples were able to feed such a large gathering with such a small amount of food, and still have plenty left over. I'm no Biblical scholar, but I do consider myself an expert on food, having eaten way yonder more than my share. I believe the disciples took those fish and that bread and made a casserole. What better way to stretch what you have?

Let's face it. Casseroles are the staple of any church dinner. They can be made ahead of time, they heat well, and they are so delicious. No one sent me a recipe for a bread and fish casserole, so I guess that one will have to remain a secret, but throughout this section of Dinner on the Grounds you will find out how to make almost every other mouth watering casserole you can think of.

Enjoy!

ASPARAGUS SUPREME

4	cups fresh OR
2	oz. pkg. frozen asparagus - sliced into 1" pieces
1	can condensed cream of shrimp soup
1/2	cup sour cream
1	tbsp. butter
1	tsp. grated onion
1/8	tsp. pepper
2	tbsp. grated carrot
1/2	cup herb seasoned stuffing mix

Cook fresh asparagus until tender. Combine soup, sour cream, onion and pepper. Fold in asparagus. Put mixture in greased dish. Add stuffing on top and sprinkle grated carrot around edge. Bake in 350 degree oven until hot and bubbly.

Louise M. Synder, Ebenezer UMC

"To everything there is a season,
and a time for every purpose under heaven.
A time to be born, and a time to die;
A time to plant, and a time to pluck up that which is planted;
A time to kill, and a time to heal;
A time to break down, and a time to build up;
A time to weep, and a time to laugh;
A time to mourn, and a time to dance . . ."

Ecclesiastes 3:1-4

BREAKFAST SOUFFLE

1   lb. sharp cheddar cheese
1/4   lb. margarine, melted (brush on bread)
White bread slices, crusts trimmed to make 2 layers

Grease a 9x13 inch pan. Grate cheddar cheese. Melt margarine. Arrange 1/2 of bread, 1/2 melted margarine and 1/2 the cheese in pan. Repeat for second layer.

7   eggs
3   cups milk
1 1/2 tsp. salt
1 1/2 tsp. worcestershire sauce
1/4   tsp. black pepper
1 1/2 tsp. dry mustard
1 1/2 tsp. paprika

Beat together and pour slowly over bread layers. Cover and re-frigerate over night. Bake uncovered at 350 degrees for 45 to 60 minutes (until set). May put crumbled bacon or cooked sausage on top during last 10 minutes of baking.   (I omit the mustard, paprika, and w. sauce.)

Serves 20.

Mary Bridges, West Rome UMC

"The earth is the Lord's, and everything in it, the world, and all who live in it . . ."

Psalm 24

BROCCOLI SOUFFLE

3   pkgs. frozen broccoli, cooked and drained
1   can cream of mushroom soup
1/2   cup mayonnaise
2   eggs, well beaten
3/4   cup grated cheese
1/4   cup grated or chopped onion
1   tsp. salt
1/2   tsp. pepper

Combine drained broccoli, soup, mayonnaise and beaten eggs. Fold in cheese, onion, salt, and pepper. Pour into greased 9x13 casserole dish. Bake 30 minutes at 375 degrees or until firm.

Frances Dean, Park Ave. UMC

BROCCOLI- CORN BAKE

1   16 oz. can cream-style corn
1   10 oz. pkg. frozen chopped broccoli
1   egg, beaten
1   Tbsp. instant minced onion
1/2   tsp. salt
Dash pepper
1/2   cup Ritz crackers, crushed
2   Tbsp. margarine, melted

Mix together. Pour into buttered one quart casserole. For a topping combine 1/2 cup Ritz cracker crumbs and 4 tablespoons of melted margarine. Sprinkle over vegetable mixture. Bake casserole uncovered at 350 degrees for 35 to 40 minutes.

Mrs. Bob (Lynn House) Gregory, North Covington Methodist Church

BROCCOLI CASSEROLE

2	pkgs. chopped broccoli, cooked & drained
3/4	cup Velveeta cheese
1	small onion, chopped
1/2	cup mayonnaise
1/2	can cream of mushroom soup
1	egg
	Ritz crackers

Combine first 6 ingredients and pour into casserole dish. Sprinkle cracker crumbs on top. Bake at 350 degrees for 20 to 25 minutes.

Mrs. Larry McIntosh, North Covington Methodist Church

MACARONI AND CHEESE

8	oz. macaroni
8	oz. cheddar cheese
2	cups milk
2	eggs
1/8	tsp. pepper

Cook macaroni according to package directions. Drain. Add remaining ingredients and cook over low heat until cheese stops sticking to spoon. Mixture firms up.

Jann Thomas, Jersey United Methodist

"Do unto others as you would have them do unto you."

Luke 6: 31

CHEESE PIE

3/4	pkg. Premium crackers
2	cups grated cheese
2	eggs
1 1/2	cup milk
1/2	stick butter

Crumble crackers. Mix 1 cup cheese together with crackers. Beat eggs and milk. Mix with crackers and cheese mixture. Place in baking dish. Sprinkle remaining cheese over top and dot with butter. Bake until egg is set.

Eunice Lively, Cedar Grove United Methodist Church

RITZ CRACKER CHICKEN

1 1/2	rolls Ritz crackers, crushed
1	stick butter or margarine, melted

Chicken pieces, bone in or boneless

Spray bottom of baking dish with non-stick spray. After washing chicken pieces, dip them in melted margarine, then roll in cracker crumbs. Place in baking dish. Cover with aluminum foil. Bake for 50 minutes. Remove the foil the last 15 minutes, so pieces become crunchy. Serve warm or cold.

Ellen Clary, Jersey United Methodist

". . . Believe in the Lord Jesus, and you will be saved--you and your household."

Acts 16: 31

15

WILD RICE CHICKEN CASSEROLE

1	lb. pork sausage
1	lb. mushrooms, sliced
2	med. onions, sliced
1	3 lb. chicken, chunked
2	cups wild rice, uncooked
1/4	cup flour
1/2	cup heavy cream
2 1/2	cups chicken broth
1	tsp. msg (optional)
	pinch of oregano, thyme, and marjoram
1	tbsp. salt
1/8	tsp. pepper

Saute sausage, remove meat. Saute onions and mushrooms. Add sausage and chicken. Cook wild rice in boiling salted water and drain. Mix flour with heavy cream until smooth. Add chicken broth and cook until thickened. Season with MSG, oregano, thyme, marjoram, salt and pepper. Combine with rice, sausage, chicken, and vegetables. Bake 25 to 35 minutes in 350 degree oven.

Serves 10.

Wednesday Night Fellowship, First Newnan UMC

"No eye has seen,
No ear has heard,
No mind has conceived
What God has prepared for those who love him."

Romans 2:9, Isaiah 64:4

CHICKEN CASSEROLE WITH YELLOW RICE

1	10 oz. pkg. yellow (Mahattma) rice
4	chicken breasts (boned and skinned)
2	cans cream of chicken soup
1	can cream of celery soup
1	stick margarine
1/2	cup water
	salt and pepper

Melt margarine in sauce pan. Add soups and water. Put uncooked rice in bottom of a large casserole dish. Pour in 1/2 the soup mixture and stir into the rice. Place the chicken halves which have been salted and peppered on top of rice mixture. Pour remainder of soups over chicken. Bake uncovered at 300 degrees for 2 hours.

Sharri Eckberg Kendrick

CHICKEN AND YELLOW RICE

1	frying chicken, cut up
1	8 1/2 oz. jar mushrooms
1	stick margarine
1	pkg. yellow rice
3	tbsp. flour
	salt and pepper

Wash chicken; salt and pepper liberally. Melt margarine in pan with well fitting lid. (I use my cast iron chicken fryer.) Put in chicken all at one time and brown fast. Then pour in mushrooms, juice and oil. Cover and simmer about 40 minutes or until tender. Twenty minutes before chicken is done, cook rice according the package directions. Place chicken on platter. Thicken broth with flour mixed with a little water. Spoon a little broth over chicken on platter. Serve rest of broth over rice.

Mrs. Rebecca Hunter, North Covington UMC

17

CHICKEN CASSEROLE

1	chicken
3	cups chicken broth
1	can cream of chicken soup
3 or 4	cups Minute rice
1/2	cup celery
1 1/3	cup onion
3/4	cup mayonnaise
	salt & pepper

Topping:

2	cups (or more) Rice Krispies
1	stick (or less) butter, melted

Boil chicken. Remove bones and skins; tear apart. Combine all ingredients. Place in casserole dish. Mix topping and spread on top. Bake 30 minutes at 350 degrees.

In memory of Mrs. Hazel Pullin, North Covington Methodist Church

CHICKEN CASSEROLE

1	chicken
2	cans cream of mushroom soup
1	8 oz. carton sour cream
1	roll Ritz crackers, crushed
1	stick butter, melted

Boil chicken and remove from bone. Combine chicken with soup and sour cream. Pour into baking dish and top with crushed Ritz crackers. Drizzle melted butter over crackers. Bake at 350 degrees for 30 minutes.

Susan (House) Hess, North Covington Methodist Church

CHICKEN CASSEROLE

1	small pkg. Uncle Ben's Wild & Long Grain Rice, cooked
1	can cream of celery soup
1	jar sliced mushrooms, drained
1/4	cup mayonnaise
2	cups cubed chicken breast, cooked (4 breast halves)
1/2	cup sour cream
1	can sliced water chestnuts
1	small jar pimentos
1	small onion, chopped
1/4	tsp. salt
1/4	tsp. pepper

Mix above ingredients. Place in casserole dish. Bake at 350 degrees for 30 minutes. Freezes well.

Bitzi Potts

CHICKEN BREASTS ON BEEF

	Chicken breasts (2 halves per person)
1	small jar of dried beef
1	can cream of chicken-mushroom soup
1	8 oz. sour cream
	Bacon slices

Place dried beef in bottom of casserole dish. Wrap each chicken breast in half a slice of bacon. Place on top of beef. Combine soup and sour cream. Pour over top of chicken. Bake <u>uncovered</u> at 300 degrees for 2 hours.

Bitzi Potts

19

CHICKEN SUPREME

3	cups coarsely chopped chicken or turkey
1	can mushroom soup
1	cup sour cream
1/2	small package Pepperidge Farm Stuffing

Combine chicken, soup, and sour cream. Put in casserole dish and cover with prepared stuffing. Bake at 350 degrees for 30-40 minutes

Suzanne Wilson, First United Methodist Church of Tucker

CRAB CASSEROLE

2	6 to 7 oz. cans crabmeat
1	cup Pepperidge Farm herb seasoned stuffing
1/2	cup milk
1/2	cup melted butter
1/2	tsp. salt
	dash pepper
1	cup grated cheddar cheese
1/2	med. size onion, chopped
1	green pepper, chopped
2	eggs, well beaten

Place all ingredients in greased casserole. Cover and bake at 325 degrees for 30 minutes.

Serves 4.

Betty Thomas, Jersey United Methodist

GRITS CASSEROLE

1 1/2	cups yellow grits
1	lb. cheese
3	eggs
1	lb. sausage, cooked and drained
	Tabasco sauce
	salt

Cook grits in 6 cups of water until done. Set aside. Mix cheese, eggs, sausage, salt and Tabasco (to taste). Mix all together and cook.

Mrs. W.D. (Jimmie N.) Gibbs, North Covington Methodist Church

BEEF & MACARONI CASSEROLE

1 1/2	lb. ground beef
1	med. onion, chopped
1	bell pepper, chopped
2	cups elbow macaroni
2	8 oz. cans tomato sauce
1	tsp. salt
1/4	tsp. pepper
2	tbsp. worcestershire sauce
1/2	cup catsup
1/2	cup water

Brown ground beef with onion and bell pepper over medium heat in large skillet. Drain off excess grease. Cook macaroni and drain. Combine beef, macaroni, and remaining ingredients. Pour into large casserole. Cover and bake at 350 degrees for 30 to 45 minutes.

Serves 6

Frances Edwards, Ebenezer UMC

HUNGRY JACK BEEF CASSEROLE

1	lb. ground beef
1	16 oz. can pork and beans
3/4	cup Kraft BBQ sauce
1	tbsp. instant minced onion
1	can (9.5 oz.) Hungry Jack biscuits
1	cup shredded Cracker Barrel cheese
1	tsp. salt
2	tbsp. brown sugar

Brown ground beef. Drain off excess grease. Combine all other ingredients except biscuits and cheese. Pour into long or round casserole dish. Cover the top with biscuits. Sprinkle with cheese. Bake 25 to 30 minutes at 375 degrees.
Serves 6.

Jane Lyle, Ebenezer UMC

PIZZA CASSEROLE

1	lb. ground beef
1	14 oz. jar pizza sauce
2	cups shredded mozzarella cheese
2	eggs
3/4	cup Bisquick
1 1/2	cup milk

Brown ground beef. Layer ground beef, pizza sauce and mozzarella cheese in 9x13 casserole dish. Whip together eggs, milk, and Bisquick. Pour over other ingredients. DO NOT STIR. Bake in a preheated oven at 400 degrees for 30 minutes or until golden brown. Kids love this!
Serves 6.

Lisa Huckaby

RICE MUSHROOM BAKE

1	cup raw rice
1	can mushrooms (any size)
1	can onion soup
1/2	can sliced water chestnuts
1	soup can water
3/4	stick margarine

Melt margarine in pyrex dish. Add other ingredients. Season to taste. Bake covered at 350 degrees for 45 to 60 minutes. (I use Basmati rice. It has a popcorn flavor which we like.)

Mary Ann Holder, Ebenezer UMC

TATERS ITALIA

2	16 oz. cans stewed tomatoes
1 1/2	tbsp. sugar
1/2	tsp. salt
1/4	tsp. basil leaves, crushed
1/8	tsp. pepper
pinch	oregano
1	16 oz. pkg. Ore-ida Tater Tots
1/3	cup cheddar cheese, grated

In large skillet over high heat, combine tomatoes and seasonings until well mixed and heated to rolling boil. Pour into 2 quart casserole. Arrange Tater Tots in a single layer on top. Bake at 425 degrees for 30 minutes or until bubbly in the center. Remove from oven and sprinkle with cheese.

Serves 6.

Wednesday Night Fellowship, First Newnan UMC

SQUASH CASSEROLE

3	pounds cooked squash
2	can cream of chicken soup
4	carrots, grated
2	small onions, chopped fine
1	stick margarine, melted
1	pkg. Pepperidge Farm dressing
8	oz. sour cream
1	medium jar pimento

Mix all ingredients except the dressing and butter. Line bottom of casserole with stuffing (save a little for top of casserole.) Add squash mixture. Top with stuffing crumbs and the melted butter. Bake at 325 degrees for 30-45 minutes.

Liz Grizzard, First United Methodist Church of Tucker

SQUASH CASSEROLE

3	lb. yellow summer squash, sliced
1/2	cup onions, chopped
2	slices of bread, toasted
1/2	tsp. black pepper
	salt to taste
2	eggs
1/2	stick margarine
1	tsp. sugar
3	tbsp. sour cream
1	cup cheddar cheese

Cook squash and onion until tender. Drain thoroughly, then mash. Add all ingredients except cheese. Pour mixture in casserole dish. Sprinkle cheese over top. Bake in 375 degree oven for approximately 1 hour. NOTE: you can substitute eggplant or zucchini squash in this recipe.

Mrs. Don (Mary) Ballard, North Covington Methodist Church

SQUASH CASSEROLE

4	med. size squash, sliced
1	cup water
1	tbsp. onion, chopped
1	tbsp. celery, chopped
1/3	cup milk
2	tbsp. grated cheese
1/3	stick margarine
1	tsp. salt
	dash of pepper
1/2	roll Ritz crackers (crushed)
1	egg, beaten

Cook squash in water until tender. Drain off water. Mash squash with fork or potato masher. Add remaining ingredients except egg and beat well. Beat egg and add to mixture. Pour into a casserole dish. Top with crushed Ritz crackers crumbs. Bake at 350 degrees for 20 to 25 minutes.

Frances Allgood, Jersey UMC

SWEET POTATO BAKE

2 - 2 1/2 lbs. sweet potatoes
1/4   cup margarine
1/4 to 1/2 cup sugar
1/4   cup raisins
1/4   cup pecans, chopped
1/3   cup miniature marshmallows

Peel and cook potatoes in water for 25 to 35 minutes or until tender. Drain, cool, then mash. Stir in butter, sugar, and raisins. Pour into large casserole dish. Sprinkle with nuts and marshmallows. Bake uncovered at 350 degrees for 30 minutes or until marshmallows are brown.

Totsie Blasingame, Jersey UMC

SWEET POTATO SOUFFLE

3	cups mashed sweet potatoes
3/4	cups butter
1/2	tsp. nutmeg
3	medium eggs, beaten
1/2	cup raisins
1 1/4	cups sugar
1	cup milk
1/2	tsp. cinnamon
2	tsp. baking powder

Combine all ingredients. Pour into a sprayed casserole dish. Bake in 400 degree oven for 20 minutes. Remove from oven and add topping. Bake another 10 minutes.

Topping:

3/4	cups cornflakes, crushed
1/2	cup brown sugar
1/2	cup pecans, chopped
3/4	stick margarine

Melt butter and mix

Mrs. W. C. (Mary Huckaby) Bouchillon, Sr., North Covington Methodist Church

"The Lord is my shepherd; I shall not want.
He maketh me to lie down in green pastures,
He leadeth me beside the still waters,
He restoreth my soul . . ."

Psalm 23: 1-3

SWEET POTATO CASSEROLE

1	16 oz. cans sweet potatoes
1	cup canned milk
3/4	stick margarine
1 1/2	cups sugar
2	eggs
dash	cinnamon

Warm potatoes and mash. Cream margarine, sugar, and eggs. Add milk, cinnamon and potatoes. Mix well. Bake in casserole dish until firm.

Topping:

2	cups corn flakes, crushed
1	cup light brown sugar
1 1/2	sticks margarine, melted
1	cup pecans, chopped

Mix together. Place on top of casserole and bake an additional 10 minutes.
Serve warm or cold.

Serves 10 to 12.

Mary Bridges, West Rome United Methodist Church

"Whatever you do, do all to the glory of God."

I Corinthians 10: 31

ZUCHINNI CASSEROLE

3	cups zuchinni, yellow, or mixed
2	eggs
2	cups seasoned cornbread crumbs
1	cup milk
1	cup grated cheese
1	cup onions, chopped
3/4	stick soft margarine
1	tsp. salt
1/4	tsp. pepper
1/2	tsp. celery salt

Cook squash and onions until tender. Drain. Combine with all other ingredients, mixing well. Bake in 11x7 casserole dish in 375 degree oven for 40 minutes.

Serves 8.

Totsie Blasingame, Jersey UMC

"Do not store up for yourselves treasures on earth, where moth and rust destroy, and where thieves break in and steal. But store up for yourselves treasures in heaven, where moths and rust do not destroy, and where thieves do not break in and steal. For where your treasure is, there your heart will be also."

Matthew 6: 19-21

The Beatitudes

"Now when he saw the crowds, he went up on a mountainside and sat down. His disciples came to him, and he began to teach them, saying:

'Blessed are the poor in spirit,
for theirs is the kingdom of heaven.
Blessed are those who mourn,
for they will be comforted.
Blessed are the meek,
for they will inherit the earth.
Blessed are those who hunger and thirst for
righteousness,
for they will be filled.
Blessed are the merciful,
for they will be shown mercy.
Blessed are the pure in heart,
for they will see God.
Blessed are the peacemakers,
for they shall be called the children of God.
Blessed are those who are persecuted because of
righteousness,
for theirs is the kingdom of heaven.'"

Matthew 5: 1-10

SOUPS, SALADS AND SUCH

"Do not work for food that spoils, but for food that endures to eternal life, which the Son of Man will give you."

John 6:27

CHAPTER TWO

I'm almost certain that bad food wasn't the focus of the preceding passage. I think Jesus was just letting us know that no matter what satisfaction we had on this earth, it was not as important as accepting God's Word and God's Son, in preparation for eternal life. But while we're here, we certainly can enjoy the earth's bounty, and folks have found some wonderful ways to preserve and prepare the food with which the Lord has blessed us.

If I close my eyes and let my mind drift back over the years I can feel the gentle autumn breeze against my face; just a tinge of crispness in the air. I can see the tables laden with good food from the larders of the people of my church; good people who worked hard, appreciated God's gifts, and made the most of his bounty.

These people tended gardens. They relied on the land to give them food and they knew how to make the most of the food they raised. Long summer evenings were spent shelling and shucking, peeling and chopping, freezing and canning and preserving. And when it was time for homecoming, on the first Sunday in October, they brought their very best to share with the members of the congregation. They brought wonderful soups and stews, all made from home grown vegetables. They brought peach pickles and pear and fig preserves, cucumber pickles of every variety, and my personal favorite, pear relish.

Of course, the table was also laden with sliced tomatoes, sliced onions, plates of hot peppers, and salads of every description.

Preserving food is becoming a lost art. People simply don't have the time or patience any more. There's far too much to do. One day, I'm afraid, we'll wake up and discover that we've lost a part of our heritage that we can never replace. Take the time to try a few of the recipes in this chapter. You'll be more than glad you did. Who knows? You may be a part of preserving our heritage.

TOMMIE HUCKABY'S BRUNSWICK STEW

2	lbs. each, cooked beef, pork, chicken
	broth from chicken and pork
4	medium potatoes
3	medium onions
2	large cans tomatoes
	juice of 1/2 lemon
2	tsp. red pepper
1	tbsp. dry mustard
1	tbsp. brown sugar
1/4	cup worscestershire sauce
1	large can whole kernel corn
1/2	lb. butter
	salt and pepper to taste

Cook meat, debone and grind. Grind potatoes and onions and cook over medium heat for 30 minutes in broth and tomatoes. Stir often to keep from sticking. Add ground meat and next 5 ingredients. Cook 30 more minutes. Add corn and butter and simmer for 20 more minutes, stirring often. Add salt and pepper to taste.

Tommie Huckaby, Julia A. Porter UMC

"Make a joyful noise unto the Lord, all ye lands,
Serve the Lord with gladness,
come before his presence with singing.
Know ye that the Lord he is God, it is he that hath made us and not
we ourselves. We are his people and the sheep of his pasture.
Enter into his gates with thanksgiving,
and into his courts with praise.
Be thankful unto him, and bless his name.
For the Lord is good, his mercy is everlasting, and his truth
endureth to all generations."

Psalm 100

33

Chicken-Vegetable Soup

1 1/2	cups chicken base
15	quarts water
3	chickens plus 1 pkg. legs & thighs, cooked, boned and cut up plus the broth
8-10	onions, chopped
5	lbs. potatoes
1	lb. carrots
4	16 oz. pkg. of frozen vegetable mixture
1	pkg. frozen string beans
1	pkg. small spaghetti
1	tbsp. thyme
1 1/2	tsp. chili powder

Add chicken and vegetables to liquid to which chicken base was added. Bring to a boil and simmer 1 1/2 hours. Add spaghetti and cook until it is tender. Add thyme and chili powder. Salt to taste. Add 1 large can tomato juice if more liquid is needed.

Freda Bullock, Park Ave. UMC

"But seek first his kingdom and his righteousness, and all these things shall be given to you as well . . .do not worry about tomorrow, for tomorrow will worry about itself . . .Ask and it will be given to you; seek and you will find; knock and the door will be opened to you. For everyone who asks, receives; he who seeks, finds; and to him who knocks, the door will be opened."

Matthew 6: 33-34, 7: 7-8

Potato Soup

2	large baking or russet potatoes
1/2	cup each of onion and celery
2	cans chicken broth
1/2	cup water
1	tsp. granulated chicken bouillon
1/2	cup cream or milk
1	tbsp. butter or margarine
	salt and pepper to taste
1	tsp. Italian seasoning (optional)

Peel and chop potatoes, onion and celery. Cook in broth and water until real soft. Mash thoroughly. Add butter, cream, salt and pepper. Heat (do not let boil), serve hot. If a creamier soup is desired, mixture can be processed in a blender.

Serves 6.

Edrie Moore, Park Ave. UMC

"Therefore everyone who hears these words of mine and puts them into practice is like a wise man who built his house on the rock. The rain came down, the streams rose, and the winds blew and beat against that house; yet it did not fall, because it had its foundation on the rock. But everyone who hears these words of mine and does not put them into practice is like a foolish man who built his house on the sand. The rain came down, the streams rose, and the winds blew and beat against that house, and it fell with a great crash."

Matthew 7: 24-27

AUNT KITTY'S BRUNSWICK STEW

1	3-4 lb. Boston butt
1	can tomatoes
1	can corn
1	stick butter
	Salt & pepper to taste
2	tbsp. sugar
1/4	cup vinegar

Boil Boston butt until done. Chop meat and combine with remaining ingredients. Simmer in broth. Thicken with small amount of bread crumbs, if necessary.

NOTE: I add 1 lb. of cooked, chopped chicken breasts.

Emily R. Barwick, Sandy Cross UMC, Crawfordville

"In the beginning was the Word, and the Word was with God, and the Word was God. The same was in the beginning with God. All things were made by him, and without him was not any thing made that was made.
In him was life, and the life was the light of men.
And the light shineth in darkness,
and the darkness comprehended it not . . .
. . . And the Word was made flesh, and dwelt among us, and we beheld his glory, the glory of the only begotten of the Father, full of grace and truth."

John 1: 1-5, 14

BRUNSWICK STEW

3 - 4	lbs. chicken
2 - 3	lbs. beef
1	lb. pork
2	qts. tomatoes
2	qts. cream style corn
3	lg. onions, chopped
2	cups catsup
2	heaping tbsp. prepared mustard
2	tbsp. sugar
1/4	cup vinegar
	Salt & pepper to taste

In 12 quart pot, boil chicken, beef and pork. Cool then bone and grind. Remove broth from pot and strain out any bone. Return 1 quart of bone-free broth to the 12 quart pot. Add all ingredients except meat and corn. Simmer until tomatoes are well done. Add ground meats. Simmer 20 to 30 minutes. Stir in fully cooked corn. If too thick, add broth or water. If too thin, thicken with bread crumbs or instant potatoes. Ready to serve or freeze in containers to open as desired.

Dorothy Parker, Jersey UMC

"Jesus answered, 'I tell you the truth, no one can enter the kingdom of God unless he is born of water and the Spirit. Flesh gives birth to flesh, but the Spirit gives birth to spirit. You should not be surprised at my saying, 'You must be born again.'"

John 3: 5-7

LEMON MAGIC

1	3 oz. pkg. lemon Jello
1	cup boiling water
2	cups soft vanilla ice cream
1	8 oz. can crushed pineapple, drained

Dissolve Jello in boiling water. Stir in ice cream into hotJello mixture. Add drained pineapple. Stir. Chill until firm and cold. Do not freeze.

Una Mae Holmgren, Jersey UMC

7 LAYER SALAD

1	box frozen green peas, thawed and uncooked
1	head lettuce, washed and broken into bite size pieces
1	green pepper, chopped
1	cup celery, chopped
4	slices bacon, cooked and crumbled
3 to 4	hard boiled eggs, chopped
1	cup cheese, grated
2	cups mayonnaise

Layer half of ingredients and repeat. Chill overnight for best results.

Una Mae Holmgren, Jersey UMC

"Be kind and loving to each other,
and forgive each other,
just as God forgave you in Christ."

Ephesians 4:32

EIGHT LAYER SALAD

1	head lettuce
1	cup chopped celery
1	cup chopped bell pepper
1	cup chopped onion
1	can English peas, drained or pkg. frozen peas
1	can sliced water chestnuts, drained
11/2	cups mayonnaise, mixed with
2	tablespoons sugar
1	cup grated cheddar cheese
6-10	strips bacon fried and crumbled or can bacos

Place lettuce in large, clear bowl. Add other vegetables and cheese in layers. Do not toss. Spread mayonnaise and sugar over top, sealing edges. Cover tightly and refrigerate at least 6 hours. When ready to serve sprinkle bacon over top. May be made the night before serving.
Serves 10-12

Renee Marrett, Conyers First UMC

"To what then can I compare the people of this generation?
They are like children sitting in the marketplace
and calling out to each other:
'We played the flute for you, and you did not dance;
We sang a dirge, and you did not cry.'
For John the Baptist came neither eating bread nor drinking
wine, and you say, 'He has a demon.' The Son of Man came
eating and drinking, and you say,
'Here is a glutton and a drunkard . . .'
But wisdom is proved right by all her children."

Luke 7: 31-35

3 BEAN MARINATED SALAD

1	No. 2 can cut green beans
1	No. 2 can cut wax beans (yellow beans)
1	No. 2 can kidney beans
1	small green bell pepper, chopped
2	stalks celery, chopped
1	med. onion, sliced and separated in rings
1/3	cup Wesson oil
1/2	cup vinegar
1/2	cup sugar

Drain all vegetables in colander. Drain kidney beans first. Pour beans, celery and pepper in bowl and mix well. Place onion rings on top. Heat oil, vinegar and sugar until sugar dissolves. Pour vinegar mixture over beans and put air tight lid on bowl. Place container in refrigerator for 24 hours. This gives plenty of time for the vegetables to marinate. Keeps well.
Serves 12 or more

Francis Allgood, Jersey UMC

". . .Martha...had a sister called Mary, who sat at the Lord's feet listening to what he said. But Martha was distracted by all the preparations that had to be made. She came to him and asked, 'Lord, don't you care that my sister has left me to do all the work by myself? Tell her to help me!' 'Martha, Martha,' the Lord answered, 'You are worried and upset about many things, but only one thing is needed. Mary has chosen what is better, and it shall not be taken away from her.'"

Luke 10: 38-42

COUNTRY POTATO SALAD

6 to 8   **cups potatoes, cooked & diced**
4   **hard cooked eggs, diced**
1/2   **cup celery, chopped**
1/4   **cup pickle relish**
1/4   **cup green onions, chopped with tops included**
1 1/2   **cups mayonnaise**
1   **tbsp. vinegar**
1/4   **tsp. white pepper**
1   **tsp. dry mustard**

Combine potatoes, eggs, celery, onions and relish in large bowl. Blend together the rest of the ingredients, then pour over potato mixture. <u>Gently</u> mix all together and chill well before serving. Garnish with parsley and sliced olives, if desired.

Marian Donley, Rincon, GA.

SWEET & SOUR GLAZED BEETS

2   **cups sliced beets, retaining 1/2 cup of juice**
1/4   **cup sugar**
1 1/2   **tbsp. corn starch**
1/4   **tsp. salt**
1/2   **cup vinegar**
1/2   **cup beet juice**
       dash of ground cloves (or 2 whole cloves)

Combine sugar, cornstarch, salt and cloves in saucepan; add vinegar and juice. Cook over medium heat, stirring constantly until thickened and bubbly. Add beets to sauce and heat for 3 to 5 minutes, stirring gently to prevent sticking.

Marian Donley, Rincon, GA

BUTTERMILK JELLO CONGEALED SALAD

1	6 oz. pkg. lime or strawberry jello
1	lg. can crushed pineapple, undrained
2	cups buttermilk
1	8 oz. container Lite Cool Whip
1	cup pecans, chopped

Combine Jello and undrained pineapple in sauce. Heat until boiling and Jello is dissolved. Remove from heat. Add buttermilk, Cool Whip, and pecans. Mix thoroughly and congeal.

Serves 10 - 12.

Edna Tanner, East Rockingham Methodist Church, North Carolina

CRANBERRY SALAD

1	lg. or 2 sm. pkg. raspberry Jello
1	cup hot water
1/2	cup cold water
1	jar Ocean Spray Cranberry-Orange relish (or plain cranberries)
1	sm. can crushed pineapple, undrained
1/4	cup walnuts, chopped

Mix jello with hot water until dissolved. Add cold water and chill until partially thickened. Fold in relish and pineapple with juices. Add walnuts and chill until set.

Freda Bullock, Park Ave UMC

"The inward man is being renewed day by day."

2 Corinthians 4:16

BUTTERSCOTCH APPLE SALAD

3 to 4	chopped apples
1	20 oz. can pineapple tidbits, undrained
1	cup raisins
1	cup miniature marshmallows
1	cup toasted pecans, chopped
1	3 oz. pkg. instant butterscotch pudding mix
1	8 oz. Cool Whip

Combine first five ingredients; sprinkle dry pudding over mixture. Fold in Cool Whip topping and mix well. Keep refrigerated.
Serves 8 - 10

Torri Frank, Ebenezer UMC

CURRIED FRUIT

1	can pineapple chunks
1	can pears
1	can sliced peaches
1	tbsp. margarine
1	cup brown sugar
2	tbsp. constarch
1/4	tsp. (mild) curry powder
1	cup reserved juice
1/4	cup maraschino cherries (optional)

Drain canned fruit (reserve pineapple juice and enough of other to make 1 cup). Cut fruit in bite-sized pieces and place in glass baking dish. In a sauce pan, mix together brown sugar, cornstarch, curry powder, margarine and juice. Heat and stir until thickened. Pour sauce over fruit. Bake uncovered at 350 degrees for 45 to 50 minutes.
Serves 10 - 12.

Frances Edwards, Ebenezer UMC

CHERRY SALAD

1	pkg. cherry Jello
3/4	cup sugar
1	can sour pie cherries
1	pkg. gelatin dissolved in 1/4 cup water
1	small can crushed pineapple
1	cup nuts, chopped (optional)
	Rind and juice of 1 lemon and 1 orange

Dissolve gelatin in cold water. Drain cherries, retaining juice. Heat juice, add sugar and Jello. Then add gelatin, nuts, pineapple, juice of orange and lemon with rind zest and cherries. Chill and pour into mold.

Mrs. Bob (Lynn House) Gregory, North Covington Methodist Church

STRAWBERRY PRETZEL SALAD

1	stick butter
2	cups broken pretzels
2	cups sugar
1	lg. pkg. strawberry Jello
2	cups boiling water
1	10 oz. pkg. frozen strawberries (unthawed)
1	8 oz. pkg. cream cheese
1	sm. can crushed pineapple, drained
1	8 oz. container Cool Whip

Sprinkle 2 tbsp. sugar in the bottom of 9x13 baking dish. Slice butter in small pieces and arrange in bottom of dish on top of sugar. Lay broken pretzels on top of butter. Bake in 350 degree oven for 15 minutes, stirring every 5 minutes, mixing pretzels, butter, and sugar. Take out of oven and cool completely. After cooling, mix cream cheese, Cool Whip, 2 cups sugar and drained pineapple. Spread on top pretzels. Refrigerate for approximately 30 minutes. Mix Jello, 2 cups boiling water, and frozen strawberries. Pour Jello mixture over cream cheese mixture. Congeal.

Ms. Susan (House) Hess, North Covington Methodist Church

CORN SALAD

1	12 oz. can shoe peg white corn
1	cup celery, chopped
1/2	cup onion, chopped
1/3	cup bell pepper, chopped (optional)
1/2	cup mayonnaise
1/2	tsp. mustard

Drain corn. Combine with all other ingredients.

In memory of Mrs. Ben House, North Covington Methodist Church

COLD VEGETABLE SALAD

1	No. 2 can shoepeg corn
1	No. 2 can French Style Green beans
1	No. 2 can tiny green peas (LeSuer)
1	cup chopped onion
1	cup chopped celery
1/2	chopped green pepper
1	small jar chopped pimento

Marinade

1	cup sugar
1/2	cup Wesson oil
2/3	cup vinegar

Drain vegetables. Mix with onion, celery, pepper, and pimento. Mix sugar, oil, and vinegar: pour over vegetables and refrigerate overnite.

Liz Grizzard, First United Methodist Church of Tucker

45

Country Tomato Salad

2	lg. tomatoes, peeled and sliced
1	cucumber, thinly sliced
1	lg. onion (sweet), thinly sliced
2	tbsp. vinegar
1 1/2	tsp. sugar
2	tbsp. cold water
1 1/2	tsp. salt

Place tomatoes, cucumbers, and onion in a shallow bowl. Combine rest of the ingredients and pour this liquid over vegetables. Chill in refrigerator at least 30 minutes before serving. (I serve mine in a 13 inch diameter shallow glass dish.) It is delicious as well as pretty.

Mrs. Rebecca Hunter, North Covington Methodist Church

Blueberry Salad

2	small pkgs. grape Jello
2	cups hot water
1	can blueberry pie filling
1	can crushed pineapple
1	8 oz. container sour cream
1	8 oz. pkg. cream cheese
1/2	cup sugar
1/2	cup Cool Whip
	vanilla (to taste)
	Nuts

Dissolve Jello in hot water. Add pie filling, crushed pineapple and mix well. Pour in pyrex dish and place in refrigerator until firm. For topping: mix cream cheese, sour cream, sugar, vanilla, nuts and Cool Whip. Spread on top of Jello mixture. Serve cool.

Mrs. W.D. (Jimmie N.) Gibbs, North Covington Methodist Church

GREEN BEAN SALAD

1	can carrots
1	can green beans
1	can kidney beans
1	can lima beans
1	bell pepper, sliced
1	onion, sliced
1/2	cup sugar
1/2	cup vinegar
1/2	cup Wesson oil

Drain all vegetables and place in large bowl. In saucepan mix sugar, vinegar, and oil. Heat to dissolve sugar. Pour over vegetables and toss. Add sliced onion and bell pepper.

Mrs. James (Kathleen) Brooking, North Covington Methodist Church

BROCCOLI SALAD

1	bunch fresh broccoli, cut up
1	med. red onion
1	cup mayonnaise
1	tbsp. vinegar
1	tbsp. sugar
1/2	cup raisins
1/2	cup sunflower seeds
4	slices bacon, cooked & crumbled

Mix all ingredients except sunflower seeds and bacon. Marinate overnight. Add seeds and stir day of serving. Top with bacon and serve.
Servings 6 to 8.

Louise Mobley, Jersey UMC

FROZEN CRANBERRY SALAD

1	16 oz. carton sour cream
2	tbsp. lemon juice
1/2	cup sugar
	dash salt
1	16 oz. can whole cranberry sauce
2	chopped bananas
1	20 oz. can crushed pineapple, drained

Combine in order given. Spoon into paper baking cups. Freeze then store in freezer bag.
Serves 16.

Jane Carter, Jersey UMC

CHINESE COLE SLAW

1   head NAPPA cabbage
5   green onions
Shred cabbage, chop onions and chill.
Lightly brown 1 stick margarine (stir constantly)
1/2 cup sesame seed
3/4 cup slivered almonds
2 pkgs. Ramen noodles, crushed (do not use noodle seasoning packet)
Sauce/Dressing
1 cup sugar
1 cup salad oil
1/2 cup vinegar
1 tsp. soy sauce
Combine in blender and beat thoroughly. About 10 minutes before serving, combine all of the above ingredients. NOTE: Mix only as much as you think you use at a time. It can be eaten later but will be soggy. Slivered almonds work better than sliced. Sliced ones become soggy.

Laverne Purser, Bonaire UMC, Bonaire, GA

Parsley Slaw

6	cups shredded cabbage
1/2	cup onion, sliced
1/2	cup green pepper, sliced
1/2	cup parsley, chopped
1/4	cup oil
1/4	cup vinegar
1/2	tsp. dry mustard
	salt to taste

Combine first 4 ingredients in large bowl. In small bowl, mix remaining ingredients well. Pour over vegetables. Cover and refrigerate 12 to 24 hours. Drain before serving.

Emily R. Barwick, Sandy Cross UMC, Crawfordville Charge

2 Cup Round Cheese Straws

2	cups grated cheese
2	sticks margarine, softened to room temperature
2	cups flour
2	cups Rice Krispies
1/2	tsp. cayenne pepper (optional)

Mix cheese and margarine together. Work in flour with hands or slow mixer. Add Rice Krispies. The batter will be very stiff. Drop batter from teaspoon and form in small balls with hands. Cook on greased cookie sheet at 350 degrees for 15 minutes or until light brown. Let cool. Store in air tight container so balls will remain crisp. Recipe will make 5 dozen.

Alice Gauntt, Jersey UMC

PEACH PICKLES

6	lbs. peeled peaches
1	tbsp. ginger
3	lbs. sugar
2	tbsp. whole cloves crushed
1	qt. vinegar
4	sticks or 4 oz. cinnamon

Peel peaches and dip into a cold salt and vinegar water solution (2tbsp. each, salt and vinegar per gallon water). Dissolve sugar in vinegar in kettle and put on range to heat. Boil 5 minutes and skim. Add spices tied in cloth bag. Wash vinegar water off peaches and drain well. Drop drained peaches into boiling syrup and cook until they can be pierced with a fork but not soft. Remove from range and allow peaches to set in syrup overnight to plump. Bring to boil and pack into jars, leaving 1/2 inch head space. Seal and process in boiling water bath for 20 minutes.

Tommie Huckaby, Julia Porter United Methodist Church

". . . Entreat me not to leave thee,
or to turn away from following after thee;
for where thou goest, I will go;
and where thou lodgest, I will lodge:
thy people shall be my people.
and thy God, my God."

Ruth 1: 16

CHEESE BALL

2	8 oz. pkg. cream cheese
.1	8 oz. can crushed pineapples (well drained)
1/4	cup finely chopped green pepper
2	tsp. finely chopped onion
1/4	cup finely chopped olives
1	tsp. seasoning salt
1	cup chopped nuts

Mix all ingredients well (reserve 1/4 cup nuts to roll cheese ball in). Refrigerate until cool before shaping and rolling in nuts to garnish.

Suzanne Wilson, FIrst United Methodist Church of Tucker

CRAB MEAT APPETIZERS

1	5 oz. jar Old English cheese spread, softened
1	6 oz. can crab meat, well drained
1	stick margarine, softened
1	tsp. onion, grated
1 1/2	tsp. mayonnaise
1/2	tsp. garlic salt
6	English muffins, split
	paprika

Spread mixture of first six ingredients on muffins. Sprinkle with paprika. Put in freeze for approx. one hour. Cut each side into wedges. Cook at 350 degrees until hot and bubbly. Can be refrozen in plastic bags prior to cooking for future use. Makes approx. 72 wedges.

Virginia Wray, Ebenezer UMC

51

SAUSAGE PINWHEELS

1	stick margarine
1	8 oz. pkg. cream cheese
2	cups self rising flour
1	lb. sausage, cooked

Cream margarine and cream cheese together. Add flour. Mix well. Shape into a ball. Roll out on floured board and spread sausage on top. Roll up into long roll. Wrap in foil and chill. Slice into pinwheels about 1/4 inch thick and bake at 400 degrees for 20 minutes.

Mrs. D. W. (Myrtle) House, North Covington Methodist Church

"If anyone would come after me, he must deny himself and take up his cross and follow me. For whoever wants to save his life will lose it, but whoever loses his life for me will save it. What good is it for a man to gain the whole world, and yet lose his own soul?"

Luke 9: 23-25

"For God so loved the world that he gave his one and only Son, that whoever believes in him shall not perish but have eternal life."

John 3: 16

REFRIGERATOR PICKLES

Use a large mouth gallon glass jug. Pack full of thinly sliced cucumbers. Mix 2 quarts water and 1 cup of salt. Pour over cucumbers and let set 4 days. Wash off, drain, put back in jug. Put in 2 tbsp. alum and cover with water. Let set 24 hours. Wash off. Put back in jug. Cover with vinegar. Let set 20 days. Wash off, drain, put back in jug and add 3 cups of sugar. Next day add 2 cups of sugar. Next day add two more cups of sugar. This makes juice. Put in containers and put in refrigerator. This will keep for two years if they last that long.

Miss Kathryn R., House, RN, North Covington Methodist Church

THREE DAY CUCUMBER OR TOMATO PICKLES

7	**lbs cucumbers or green tomatoes**
2	**cups lime**
2	**gal. water**
5	**lbs. sugar**
1 1/2	**tsp. pickling spice**
3	**pints vinegar**

1st day - Wash and slice 7 lbs. cucumbers or green tomatoes. Mix 2 cups lime and 2 gallons water and soak for 24 hours.

2nd day - Drain lime water and wash 2 or 3 times and soak in clear water for 4 hours.

Mix 5 lbs. sugar, less 1 1/2 cups, 1 1/2 tsp. pickling spice (tie in rag and place in mixture) and 3 pints of vinegar. Dissolve and bring to a boil. Put cucumbers or tomatoes in syrup; turn off and let soak overnight.

3rd day- Bring to a boil then turn down on low. Cook 30 minutes. Have jars clean with new lids. Place pickles in jars, cover with mixture, seal, set upside down for 24 hours.

In memory of Mrs. Jack (Allie B.) Gibbs, North Covington Methodist

FROZEN CUCUMBER PICKLES

2   qts. cucumbers, thinly sliced
5   onions, thinly sliced
2   tbsp. salt
1   cup white vinegar
3   cups sugar

Put first 3 ingredients in pan and let stand for 2 hours; stir often and then drain liquid off. Mix vinegar and sugar, heat just enough to melt sugar. Pack cucumbers in 1/2 pint containers and pour syrup over them. Freeze.

NOTE: Mrs. Ben House experimented with "Miss Mary's" recipe using yellow squash and green tomatoes. They both were delicious also.

Mrs. W. C. (Mary Huckaby) Bouchillon Sr., North Covington Methodist

JACK RAWLS CHILE

2   lbs. ground chuck
2   tbsp. butter
2   cans (No. 2) tomatoes
2   tbsp. chili powder
2   tbsp. prepared mustard
2   medium onions, chopped
2   cans kidney beans
    pepper, salt, red pepper, Tabasco sauce

Brown beef and onions in butter. Add other ingredients. Simmer for one hour and eat, with cornbread, sliced onions and red peppers, at your own risk.

Darrell Huckaby, Porterdale

Cinnamon Cucumber Rings or Strips

2	gal. large cucumbers (larger the better, even old yellow ones) approx. 15 cukes
2	cups dehydrated lime
8 1/2	quarts water
1	cup apple vinegar
2	bottles (1 oz. sized) red food coloring
1	tbsp. alum
	Additional water

Cut cukes in 1/4 inch rings or strips.. Remove seeds and centers with melon cutter. Put lime in water. Add cukes. Let stand overnight; drain. Wash thoroughly in cold water. Pour cold water over cukes. Soak, covered with ice for 3 hours. Drain; add vinegar, food coloring and alum with water to cover. Simmer just below boil for 2 hours. Drain.
Make a syrup as follows:

6	cups apple vinegar
6	cups water
7 1/2	lbs. sugar
15 +	cinnamon sticks, crushed
1	8 oz. pkg. red hots (candy)

Mix well and bring to a boil, dissolving all red hots and pour over cukes. Let stand overnight. Drain and reheat the red syrup. Pour over rings for two nights. On third morning, heat both rings and syrup. Pack into sterilized jars and seal. Yield: approximately 5 quarts.

Melba Mathis
Earline Cole

VEGETABLES

"Then God said, 'I give you every seed bearing plant on the face of the earth and every tree that has fruit with seed in it. They will be yours for food. . . . I give every green plant for food.' "

Genesis 1: 29-30

CHAPTER THREE

I'm here to tell you, God knew what he was doing when he gave us vegetables to eat. What a wonderful idea! In the spring of the year, when the air and the ground are warming up, making you want to get outside and play in the dirt, anyway, you get to go outside and break up the ground.

A fellow with a mule and hand held plow used to do ours. I guess the guy's mule died because he showed up one spring with a gasoline powered rotary tiller. My daddy figured he could use one of those and bought one the next year. From then on, he did his own plowing.

What a simple process. Get the ground nice and smooth, drop in a few seeds and scatter a little cow manure. I bet politicians would make good farmers. They sure do know how to spread the manure.

After the planting is done the spring rains cause plants to spring forth from the ground. By the time summer's here and the days are long enough to work outside after supper, those plants are producing wonderful food—peas, butterbeans, corn, squash, tomatoes, cucumbers, okra—I could go on and on.

You know, there are some poor souls in this world who are educated beyond their intelligence. They will tell you stories of a great evolution and try to convince you to discount the creation. They claim that all life on earth sprang forth because two lifeless meteors crashed into one another a zillion years ago.

Brothers and sisters, I'm here to tell you that corn and okra didn't happen by accident. I'm also here to tell you that folks in the South have come up with some wonderful ways to cook all those marvelous vegetables we grow. Try these recipes out and you'll understand why some people are able to sustain themselves as vegetarians.

BAKED BEANS

1	3 lb. can pork and beans
1	med. onion, chopped
1/2	cup bell pepper, chopped
4	tbsp. worcestershire sauce
1/2	cup dark brown sugar, packed
1	tbsp. mustard
1/4	cup ketchup
	bacon strips

Mix together all the ingredients and pour in a baking dish. Place strips of bacon on top and bake at 375 degrees for one hour.

Mrs. Russell (Terri House) Barksdale, North Covington Methodist Church

BAKED BEANS

1	16 oz. can kidney beans
1	16 oz. can butter beans
1	16 oz. can pork & beans
8	strips of bacon, cut in 1/4" pieces
1	large onion, diced
1/4	cup vinegar
1/2	tsp. dry mustard
3/4	cup brown sugar

Drain the juice from all beans. Brown bacon until crisp, drain grease. Saute onion. Add vinegar, dry mustard and brown sugar. Simmer 15 minutes. Add sauce to beans in ovenproof crockpot. Bake at 350 degrees for 1 hour.

Julie Reed, Asbury UMC, Janesville, WI

59

UKRANIAN BBQ BEANS

1	can kidney beans
1	can green beans
2	cans pork & beans
3-4	lg. onions, sliced into rings
1/4	cup cider vinegar
1	cup brown sugar
8	slices of bacon
2	cloves garlic, minced

Drain all beans. Fry bacon, drain and set aside. Add onion rings, brown sugar, vinegar, and garlic to bacon drippings. Simmer 20 minutes in fry pan. Combine all beans and mix in large bowl. Add onion mixture and crumbled bacon. Bake at 350 degrees for 1 hour.

Louise M. Snyder, Ebenezer UMC

GRANNY BEANS

1 1/2	lb. ground beef or turkey, browned
2	cans butter beans, drained
2	cans pork and beans
2	cans kidney beans
1	cup brown sugar
1	cup white sugar
1	cup ketchup
1	tsp. dry mustard
1	onion, chopped

Mix all ingredients and bake for 1 1/2 hours at 325 degrees.

Cheryl Hancock, Oak Grove United Methodist Church

CORN PUDDING

1	can creamed corn
2	can whole corn, drained
2	tbsp. melted margarine
1	cup milk
1	tsp. sugar
2	eggs
	salt & pepper

Melt margarine and heat milk. Add salt and pepper. Beat eggs. Add 2 tbsp. hot milk into eggs. Stir then add to hot milk and margarine. Place into greased baking dish. Stir in creamed and whole corn. Bake uncovered at 350 degrees for 1 1/2 hours. This is a family favorite!

Serves 9.

Peg Rosing

COUNTRY FLAVOR GREEN BEANS

	Fresh green beans
1/2	tsp. sugar
1	tbsp. salt
	Small piece of salt pork

Prepare beans. Wash in cold water. Add enough cold water to cover beans. Add salt, sugar, and salt pork. Cook 3 1/2 hours on medium heat. Boil dry before serving. You may prepare lima beans or fresh peas in same way.

Mary Akin, Ebenezer UMC

"God . . . richly furnishes us with everything to enjoy."

1 Timothy 6: 17

THREE BEAN BAKE - ONE DISH PREP

6	slices bacon
2	med. onions, sliced & separated in rings
1	16 oz. can baked beans
1	16 oz. can butter beans, drained
1	8 1/2 oz. can lima beans, drained
1/4	cup brown sugar, packed
1/4	cup chili sauce
3	tbsp. vinegar
1	tbsp. prepared mustard

Arrange bacon in a 2 qt. microwave casserole. Cover with microwave safe paper towels. Cook on high (100% power) 4 to 7 minutes until crisp. Remove bacon, reserving 1 tbs. of drippings. Drain bacon on paper towels, crumble and set aside. Add onion rings to reserved drippings in casserole. Cook, covered on high 3 to 5 minutes until onion is tender, stirring once. Drain well. In same dish, combine bacon, onion rings, undrained baked beans, drained lima beans and butter beans, brown sugar, chili sauce, vinegar and mustard. Cook, uncovered on high 11 to 13 minutes until heated through, stirring once.

Makes 6 servings.

Margaret Thompson, Smyrna First UMC

"Come unto me, all who labor and are heavy laden, and I will give you rest. Take my yoke upon you , and learn from me; for I am gentle and lowly in heart, and you will find rest for your souls. For my yoke is easy, and my burden is light."

Matthew 11: 28-30

DELICIOUS VIDALIA ONIONS

3	Vidalia onions
2	cups water
1	cup sugar
1/2	cup white vinegar

Separate sliced onions into rings. Mix with other ingredients. Refrigerate 5 hours or overnight. Drain well and mix with may-onnaise to coat. Sprinkle with celery seed or celery salt. Serve while cold.

Mary Akin, Ebenezer EMC

BAKED VIDALIA ONIONS

1/2	cup crushed peanuts
1	tbsp. margarine
4	large Vidalia onions, peeled and quartered
1/2	cup beef stock
1	tsp. salt
1	tsp. pepper
2	tsp. celery salt
3	tbsp. margarine
2	tbsp. flour

Saute peanuts in 1 tbsp. margarine until hot and cooked through. Remove peanuts and set aside. In same pan, lightly brown on-ions on cut sides. Add stock, salt, pepper and celery salt. Cover and let simmer until onions are translucent (12 minutes)
In separate pan, melt 3 tbsp. margarine and whisk in the flour. Drain off liquid from onions and place onions in baking dish. Add liquid to flour and margarine mixture, beating until smooth. Add the peanuts to this sauce. Pour the sauce over the onions in the baking dish. Bake at 350 degrees until sauce bubbles (about 10 minutes).

In memory of Miss Eva Mask, North Covington Methodist

VIDALIA ONION AU GRATIN

6	large Vidalia onions, sliced in 1/4 inch pieces
2	tbsp. margarine
1/3	cup water
1/3	cup flour
1/2	lb. grated cheddar cheese
1/3	cup milk
	bread crumbs; salt and pepper to taste

Peel and slice onions, cut in 1/4 inch slices. Add margarine to large fry-pan. When melted, add onions and water. Salt and pepper to taste. Cover and cook until tender-crisp. Add flour and stir in well. Add grated cheddar cheese and milk. Cook until bubbly and cheese is melted. Put in greased casserole and top with more cheese or bread crumbs. Bake at 325 degrees about 15-20 minutes.

Rev. David Hancock, Oak Grove United Methodist Church

VIDALIA ONION PIE

3	medium Vidalia onions
1/2	cup butter
3	eggs, lightly beaten
1	cup low-fat sour cream
1/4	tsp. salt
1/2	tsp. pepper
1/4	tsp. cayenne red pepper
1	9-inch pie shell, unbaked
1/2	cup grated parmesan cheese

Preheat oven to 450 degrees. Thinly slice onions, cutting each slice into quarters. Saute onions in butter until soft and transparent. Combine eggs, sour cream, salt, pepper and cayenne red pepper until smooth. Place onions in pie shell. Pour egg mixture over onions. Sprinkle with cheese. Bake at 450 degrees for 15 minutes. Lower oven to 325 degrees and bake another 15 to 20 minutes until lightly brown and set. Serve warm. Serves 8.

Mark Akin, Ebenezer UMC

BEAN CASSEROLE

1	can french style green beans
1	can mushroom soup
1/2	can water
1	can french fried onions

Drain beans and spread in dish. Mix soup and water and bring to a boil. Pour over beans and cook 25 minutes in a 350 degree oven. Spread onions over mixture and let brown lightly.

Mrs. Russell (Terri House) Barksdale, North Covington Methodist Church

POTATO CASSEROLE

2	pkgs. frozen hash brown potatoes, thawed
1	can cream of chicken soup
1	small onion, chopped
1/2	stick margarine, melted
1	16 oz. container sour cream
2	cups cheddar cheese, grated
1	tsp. salt
1/4	tsp. pepper

Mix all ingredients in large bowl. Pour into large casserole. Make a topping of 2 cups crushed corn flakes mixed with 1/4 cup melted butter. Bake at 350 degrees for 45 minutes. Freezes well.

Lisa Huckaby, Ebenezer UMC

**"... if serving the Lord seems undesirable to you, then choose for yourselves this day whom you will serve, . . .
But as for me and my household, we will serve the Lord."**

Joshua 24: 15

HASH BROWN OMELET

4	slices bacon
2	cups shredded, cooked potatoes or frozen hash browns, cooked
1/4	cup minced onion
1/4	cup finely chopped green pepper
4	eggs
1/4	cup milk
1/2	tsp. salt
	dash pepper
1	cup (4 oz.) shredded American or cheddar cheese

In skillet, fry bacon over medium-low heat until crisp. Drain bacon and crumble. Leave bacon drippings in skillet. Combine potatoes, onion, and green pepper. Pat evenly in skillet. Cook over low heat until underside is crisp and brown, about 6 minutes. In mixing bowl, blend eggs, milk, salt and pepper. Pour over potatoes. Top with cheese and crumbled bacon. Cover and cook over low heat, about 4 minutes. When egg is done, loosen omelet. Fold in half. Makes 4 servings.

Janet Walton, County Line United Methodist, Griffin

PINEAPPLE CRISP

2	large cans pineapple in own juice drained
3/4	cup sugar
1/4	cup brown sugar
5	tbsp. flour
1	stick margarine
1 1/2	cups cheddar cheese, grated
1	cup Ritz cracker crumbs

Butter 9x13 casserole. Place pineapple in bottom. Mix sugar and flour, spread over pineapple. Sprinkle cheese and cracker crumbs over mixture. Pour melted margarine over top. Bake at 350 degrees for 30 minutes.

Wednesday Night Fellowship, First UMC Newnan

CONSOMME RICE

1	cup rice
1	large onion, chopped
1/2	stick margarine
1	small can of mushrooms
2	cans consomme soup
	salt & pepper to taste

Brown rice in the margarine. When brown, add chopped onion to rice. Add 2 cans of consomme soup and mushrooms. Salt and pepper to taste. Bake in a casserole dish at 325 degrees for one hour

Laura Osiecki

EASY BAKED RICE

1	stick margarine
1 1/2	cups Uncle Ben' s converted rice
1	can beef consomme soup
1	can French onion soup
1	large can mushroom

Melt butter with beef consomme and onion soup. Mix all other ingredients and place in a covered container. Bake 1 hour at 350 degrees. Fluff with fork when ready to serve.

Ann W. Brooks, Jersey UMC

"By wisdom the Lord laid the earth's foundations,
by understanding he set the heavens in place;
by his knowledge the deeps were divided,
and the clouds let drop the dew."

Proverbs 3:19-20

SQUASH SOUFFLE

2	cups cooked squash, mashed
1	cup bread crumbs
1	cup sweet milk
3	tbsp. butter
3	eggs, beaten
1	cup grated cheese
	salt & pepper to taste

Heat milk and add butter. Pour over bread crumbs. Mix well and add to the squash and cheese. Let cool slightly. Add eggs and seasonings. Pour into a buttered casserole dish. Top with Ritz cracker crumbs. Bake at 350 degrees for 1 hour or until set.

Serves 8

Frances McKissick, Jersey UMC

SCALLOPED TOMATOES

6	medium sized tomatoes
4	strips bacon
2	hard cooked eggs, sliced thin
2	cups cracker crumbs
1/2	cup hot water
	bacon drippings
	salt & pepper
1/2	cup grated cheese

Fry bacon crisp, saving drippings for seasoning. Peel and slice tomatoes. In a 1 quart casserole, place a layer of tomatoes, part of crumbled bacon and sliced egg. Add salt and pepper, then a layer of cracker crumbs. Repeat layers ending with tomatoes. Add some bacon drippings to hot water and pour over tomatoes. Top with cheese. Take at 325 degrees for 30 minutes.

Mrs. Olin (Runell) Allen, North Covington Methodist

BROCCOLI AND RICE CASSEROLE

1/2	stick margarine
1/2	cup celery, chopped
1/4	cup onion, chopped
1	10 oz. pkg. frozen broccoli, cooked with salt
2 1/2	cups cooked rice
1	small jar Cheez Whiz
1	can cream of chicken soup
	Tabasco sauce and pepper to taste

Saute onions and celery in margarine. Combine with all remaining ingredients. Place in a large casserole dish. Bake uncovered at 350 degrees for 45 minutes.

Lisa Huckaby

*"The king of Egypt said to the Hebrew midwives . . .
'When you help the Hebrew women in childbirth . . . if it is a
boy, kill him; but if it is a girl, let her live.' The midwives,
however, feared God and did not do what the king of Egypt
had told them to do; they let the boys live. . .
So God was kind to the midwives and the people increased
and became even more numerous. And because the midwives
feared God, he gave them families of their own."*

Exodus 1: 16, 20-21

*"Train a child in the way he should go,
and when he is old he will not turn from it."*

Proverbs 22: 6

69

ENTREES

"There, in the presence of the Lord your God, you and your families shall eat and shall rejoice in everything you have put your hand to, because the Lord you God has blessed you."

Deuteronomy 12:7

CHAPTER FOUR

My mama didn't live an easy life. She was raised by her mother during the Great Depression. I don't think the people of rural Georgia knew there was a depression going on. They just knew it was hard times. My mother never had a lot of material things. Her mother, my grandmother, Mama Ellis, got by and provided for her family as best she could.

It has been evident to me my whole life that one thing my mother was not deprived of as a child was love. She must have been given an abundance of love, because she had an awful lot of it to give away to her friends and family.

My mama cooked the best fried chicken in the whole world. There's no room for discussion about the issue. Cooking that fried chicken was one way my mama had of bestowing her love on her family. She would fix it for us on all the special days of our lives. I was nearly forty years old before I learned that it was possible to go on an overnight trip in an automobile without a shoebox full of Mama's fried chicken in the back seat. I wish I had never made that discovery.

When it came time for dinner on the grounds at the Porterdale Methodist Church, you can rest assured you'd never see a red and white bucket of chicken on the table. The platters of chicken were all freshly fried in the kitchens of Porterdale— with great love. There's no way to count the number of platters of Southern fried chicken Tommie Huckaby brought to church dinners, but I can tell you with great certainty the number of pieces that she brought back home with her. None.

Her recipe is not the only one for an entree or main dish in this chapter, but it's the best. Be sure to remember to season with love. That's the most important ingredient.

PORTERDALE FRIED CHICKEN

1   fryer Cut-up
     salt
2   cups milk
2   cups plain flour
     cooking oil

Cut up, skin, and wash a fryer size chicken. Rub with salt. Soak 20 minutes in sweet milk. Drain, then dredge with flour. Fry in oil at 360 degrees until done. Turn once when brown. Cover skillet with lid and turn heat down to slow simmer. When done, drain on paper towel.

Tommie Huckaby, Julia Porter UMC

BARBECUE CHICKEN

1   can Coca Cola or Diet Coke
1/2 cup ketchup
1   medium onion
2   tbs. worcestershire sauce
1   (2 1/2 - 3 lb.) chicken, cut up

Mix ingredients, slice onion in thin slices, add chicken and cook on top of stove. Bring to a boil, then reduce heat. Cook until almost done. Turn on high to cook sauce down until thick. Pork chops are delicious cooked by this recipe also.

Miss Kathryn R. House RN, North Covington Methodist Church

". . . Jesus called the children to him and said,
'Let the little children come unto me, and do not hinder them,
for the kingdom of God belongs to such as these.'"

Luke 18: 16

CHICKEN ENCHILADAS

1	dz. corn tortillas
	cooked chicken, cut up
	diced onion
	grated Monterey Jack Cheese
1	can chicken broth
1	cup sour cream (do not use nonfat sour cream)
2	tbsp. flour
	cumin
	chili powder
	salt & pepper

Warm the tortillas. Place some chicken, onion and cheese in a tortilla. Roll up the tortilla and place in a 8x11 inch baking dish seam side down. Repeat with rest of tortillas. In a small pot, heat chicken broth to boiling. In a bowl, thoroughly whisk flour into sour cream, then stir mixture into the hot broth. Season the sauce lightly with cumin, chili powder, salt and pepper to taste. Pour sauce over filled tortillas. Bake at 350 degrees for 30 minutes. Serve with sour cream and salsa.

Roberta Wilson, Jersey UMC

CHICKEN ROLL-UPS

4	chicken breasts
1	can cream of chicken soup
1	stick margarine, melted
1	can crescent rolls
1/2	cup milk
1	cup grated mild cheddar cheese

Boil chicken breasts and remove meat from bones. Flatten crescent rolls and fill with chicken and roll. Mix soup, milk, margarine and cheese. Place chicken rolls in casserole and cover with sauce. Bake uncovered for 30 minutes at 350 degrees.

Lisa Huckaby

DEEP FRIED CHICKEN

1	(2 1/2 lb.) frying chicken, cut into 6 - 8 serving pieces
1	cup water
1/2	cup plain flour
2	tsp. salt
1/4	tsp. pepper
1	egg
2	tbsp. water
3/4	cup fine bread crumbs.
	Crisco for deep frying

In a pot with a tight cover, place chicken on rack and cover with 1 cup of water. Bring water to a boil, cover and steam 20 to 25 minutes. Shake steamed chicken pieces in a paper bag containing flour, salt and pepper. Beat egg and water together. Dip floured chicken in egg mixture, then roll in fine bread crumbs. Allow to stand about 10 minutes to let coating set. Fry in deep Crisco heated to 365 degrees until brown and crispy, about 3 to 5 minutes. Drain on paper towels before serving.

Mrs. Frances Wander, North Covington Methodist Church

"Whoever watches the wind will not plant;
whoever looks at the clouds will not reap . . .
Sow your seed in the morning, and at evening
let not your hands be idle, for you do not know
which will succeed, whether this or that,
or whether both will do equally well."

Ecclesiastes 11:4, 6

SOUTHERN DRESSING

1/2	cup onion, chopped fine
1/2	cup celery, chopped fine
3	eggs
	salt & pepper
1	tsp. poultry seasoning
	cooked cornbread (8x8 size), crumbled
	cooked biscuits (8 to 10), crumbled
	chicken broth to moisten

Combine all ingredients in large bowl. Bake at 350 degrees for 45 minutes or until lightly brown. Make a giblet gravy by boiling giblets in broth. Chop when done. Add back to broth along with chopped boiled egg. Thicken broth with flour.

Tommie Huckaby, Julia Porter UMC

EASY CHICKEN AND RICE

1	cup regular rice, uncooked
1	10 3/4 oz. can cream of mushroom soup, undiluted (may substitute cream of chicken)
2-3/4	cups water
1	2 or 3 pound chicken, cut up
1/2	teaspoon salt
1/8	teaspoon pepper
2	tablespoons butter or margarine, cut into 1/8 inch slices.

Sprinkle rice in 13 x 9 baking dish. Combine soup and water; pour over the rice.

Place chicken pieces, skin side up, in baking dish; Sprinkle with salt and pepper.

Place a piece of butter on each piece of chicken.

Bake at 350 degrees for 1 hour.

6 servings.

Lorraine Simpson, Garden City

AMA'S SPAGHETTI SAUCE

3	small cans tomato paste
1	15 oz. can tomato sauce
1	large onion, chopped
4	garlic cloves, minced
1	lb. ground beef
2	paste cans of water

Brown beef, draining grease. Add remaining ingredients. Cook on low for at least 30 minutes.

Jane Carter, Jersey UMC

ITALIAN TOMATO MEAT SAUCE

1	lb. ground beef
2	15 oz. cans plain tomato sauce
2	15 oz. cans diced tomatoes, drained
4	tbsp. tomato paste
1/2	cup onion, diced
1/2	cup mushrooms, sliced
1	clove minced garlic
1	tsp. dried basil
1/2	tsp. dried oregano
1/4	tsp. dried thyme
	salt & pepper to taste

In a large pot, brown ground beef, draining off all grease. Add tomatoes, tomato sauce, tomato paste, onions, mushrooms and garlic. Simmer uncovered for 30 minutes, stirring occasionally. Add basil, oregano, thyme, salt & pepper. Serve with hot pasta. Leftover sauce freezes well.
Serves 8.

Roberta Wilson, Jersey UMC

LASAGNA

1   lb. ground beef
1   medium onion, chopped
1   jar Italian cooking sauce
1   small can tomato paste
1   large can tomato sauce
1   small container cottage cheese
    sliced muenster cheese
    sliced mozzarella cheese
    parmesan cheese
    lasagna noodles

Brown ground beef with onions. Drain grease. Add Italian cooking sauce, tomato sauce, tomato paste and cottage cheese. Let simmer. Cook noodles and drain. In casserole dish, layer sauce, noodles, and cheeses. Sprinkle parmesan cheese on top. Bake at 400 degrees for 35 to 40 minutes.

Ms. Susan (House) Hess, North Covington Methodist Church

"Therefore, since we are surrounded by such a great cloud of witness, let us throw off everything that hinders and the sin that so easily entangles, and let us run with perseverance the race marked out for us. Let us fix our eyes upon Jesus, the author and perfecter of our faith, who for the joy set before him endured the cross, scorning its shame, and sat down at the right hand of the throne of God."

Hebrews 12: 1-2

MOTHER'S SPAGHETTI

1 1/2	lbs. ground beef
1	large onion, chopped
1	green pepper, chopped
1	garlic clove, chopped
8	oz. mushrooms, chopped
2	6 oz. cans tomato paste
1	8 oz. can tomato sauce
1	16 oz. can tomatoes
1	cup water
1	tbsp. Italian seasoning
1	tbsp. worcestershire sauce
2	tbsp. sugar
1	tsp. salt

Brown meat, onions, green pepper and garlic clove in large Dutch oven. Drain all grease. Add all other ingredients. Simmer 1 hour. Serve other spaghetti noodles with large tossed salad and garlic bread.
Serves 6 to 8

Alice Jo Giddens, Park Avenue UMC

"And Jesus came and spoke to his disciples saying, 'All power is given unto me in heaven and earth. Go therefore, and teach all nations, baptizing them in the name of the Father and of the Son, and of the Holy Ghost: Teaching them to observe all things whatsoever I have commanded you; and lo, I am with you always, even unto the end of the world."

Matthew 28: 18-20

HAMBURGER HASH

1- 1 1/2 pounds ground beef. (browned and drained)
1   cup celery, cut
1   medium onion, cut
3/4   cup rice (uncooked Uncle Ben's- not instant
1   can cream mushroom soup
1   can cream chicken soup
1/4   cup soy sauce
1 1/2   cups warm water
1/8   teaspoon pepper

Mix all together. Bake 1 1/2 hours at 325 degrees. Put 1 can Chinese noodles over top and bake 15 minutes longer. No extra salt needed.

Suzanne Wilson, First United Methodist Church of Tucker

HAMBURGER STROGANOFF

1/4   cup margarine
1/2   cup onion, minced
1   lb. ground beef
1   garlic clove, minced
2   tbsp. flour
1/4   tsp. MSG
2   tbsp. parsley, minced
1/4   tsp. pepper
8   oz. can mushrooms, sliced
1   cup sour cream
2   tsp. salt
1   can cream of chicken soup, undiluted

In hot margarine, saute onions until golden. Stir in meat, garlic, flour, salt, MSG, pepper, and mushrooms. Saute 5 minutes. Add soup; simmer uncovered 10 minutes. Stir in sour cream; heat; sprinkle with parsley. Serve on hot mashed potatoes, fluffy rice, buttered noodles or toast.

Una Mae Holmgren, Jersey UMC

CABBAGE STEW

1/2   lb. ground beef
2   cans stewed tomatoes
2   cans pinto beans
2   cans water
1   tbsp. chili powder
1   medium cabbage, shredded
    salt & pepper

Mix all ingredients in large container. Cook for 1 to 1 1/2 hours. Serve with cornbread.

Peggy Price, Hartwell

MEXACALI MEAT LOAF

1 1/2   lbs. ground beef
1/2-3/4 cup Pace picante sauce
1   slice bread, crumbled
1   egg, slightly beaten
    dash of salt & pepper

Combine all ingredients together. Shape into loaf. Place in glass loaf pan. Cook in microwave on 160 degrees or high for 20 minutes. <u>Sauce:</u> 3/4 cup ketchup, 1/4 cup brown sugar, 2 tbsp. mustard, and 3 tbsp. worcestershire sauce. Cover meat loaf w/ sauce prior to baking.

Serves 6

Jane Carter, Jersey UMC

"Let your light so shine before men, that they may see your good works, and glorify your Father which is in heaven."

Matthew 5: 16

BBQ MEAT LOAF

3	lbs. ground beef
1	cup ketchup
2	medium onions, chopped fine
2	cups bread crumbs
2	eggs
1	tbsp. brown sugar
1/2	cup water
	salt & pepper to taste

Combine all ingredients, mixing well. Place in baking dish. Will make 2 loaves. Cook in BBQ sauce. Spoon sauce over meat every 30 minutes until meat is done. Cook 1 1/2 hours at 400 degrees. <u>BBQ sauce:</u> 1 1/2 cups ketchup, 1/2 cup water, 3 tbsp. worcestershire sauce, 3 tbsp. prepared mustard, 3 tbsp. sugar.

Mary Akin, Ebenezer UMC

BEEF STOGANOFF

1 1/2	cups cooked beef, cut into strips
1	can mushroom soup
1/2	tsp. rosemary
2	tbsp. sour cream
1	onion, chopped
1	cube beef bouillon
	dash of salt & pepper

Heat meat in non-stick skillet. Add onion and cook for 2 minutes. Add soup, bouillon and spices. Cook until warm and bubbly. Remove from heat and add sour cream. Serve over hot cooked noodles.

Jann Thomas, Jersey UMC

BEEF PORCUPINES

1	lb. ground beef
1/2	cup raw rice
1/4	cup chopped onion
1	tsp. salt
1/4	tsp. pepper
2	tbsp. cooking oil
2	8oz. cans tomato sauce
1	cup water

Mix beef, rice, onions, and seasonings. Form into small balls. Fry in hot oil, turning frequently, until light brown but not crusty on all sides. Add tomato sauce and water. Mix well. Cover and simmer about 45 minutes. Makes 4 servings.

Lorraine Simpson, Garden City, GA

CROCK POT BEEF TIPS

1	lb. stew beef
1	can cream of mushroom soup
1	can celery soup
1	pkg. dry Lipton onion soup
1/4	cup water

Trim and cut meat into bite-size pieces. Combine all soups and water, stirring well. Add meat to mixture and stir well. Cook on low in crock pot for 6 to 8 hours. Serve over egg noodles or rice.

Serves 2 or 3

Sharri Echberg Kendrick, Marietta

SHERRIED BEEF

3	lb. boneless chuck roast
1	pkg. Lipton dry onion soup
2	cans mushroom soup
3/4	cup sherry

Cut roast into 1" cubes. Combine all ingredients. Place in 3 quart casserole. Cover and bake 3 hours in 325 degree oven. Serve with rice or noodles. This recipe is easy and delicious!

Serves 6

Betty Thomas, Jersey UMC

CROCK POT TURKEY BARBECUE

5 or 6	turkey thighs, skinned
1	oz. jar Heinz 57 sauce
2	tbsp. dry mustard
1	tsp. vinegar
1	small onion, chopped
1/2	tsp. salt
1/2	tsp. black pepper

Place all ingredients in crock pot. Cook for 8 hours. Remove bones and pull meat apart. Leave in crock pot to absorb juices.

Edith C. Sanders, Hartwell, GA

"Think not that I have come to destroy the law,
or the prophets:
I am not come to destroy, but to fulfil."

Matthew 5: 17

HAM CASSEROLE

2	cups ham, cooked and cubed
2	cups rice, cooked
1/2	cup cheese, grated
1/2	cup evaporated milk
1	can cream of mushroom or celery soup
4	tbsp. onion, chopped
3/4	cups corn flakes, crushed
3	tbsp. melted butter

Combine all ingredients and put in greased casserole dish. Top with corn flakes and butter. Bake 30 minutes at 375 degrees. Serves 6 to 8.

Frances Dean, Park Ave. UMC

SALMON LOAF

3	6 oz. cans Chicken of Sea boneless salmon
1/2	cup Miracle Whip salad dressing
1	can cream of chicken soup
1	cup bread crumbs
1	egg
1/2	cup onion, chopped
1/4	cup green pepper, chopped
1	tbsp. lemon juice
1	tsp. salt

Drain and flake salmon. Combine with remaining ingredients and mix well. Place in loaf pan. Bake 1 hour in 350 degree. Serves 6 to 8.

Susan W. Smith, Ebenezer UMC

85

SALMON LOAF

1	lb. can salmon
1	cup corn flakes
2	eggs
1	cup milk
1/4	tsp. salt
	dash pepper

Drain and debone salmon. Combine with other ingredients. Cover with buttered, crushed corn flakes. Bake for 30 minutes in 350 degree oven.

Serves 4

Betty Thomas, Jersey UMC

RITZ FISH

8 to 10 fresh fish fillets

1	tube Ritz crackers
1/4	cup parmesan cheese
1/2	stick butter, melted

Crush crackers. Dip fish fillets in margarine, then coat well with cracker mixture. Place on foil lined pan, sprayed with Pam. Drizzle remaining margarine over fish. Sprinkle with cheese. Bake 20 minutes at 450 degrees.

Torri Frank, Ebenezer UMC

"And he will send his angels with a loud trumpet call, and they will gather his elect from the four winds, from one end of heaven to the other."

Matthew 24: 31

MARYLAND CRAB CAKES

1	lb. white crab meet
3 to 4	bread slices, crumbled
1	large egg
1/4	cup mayonnaise
1/2	tsp. salt
1/4	tsp. pepper
1	tsp. Old Bay seasoning
1	tsp. dry mustard

Remove all cartilage from crab meat. In bowl, mix bread crumbs, egg, mayonnaise and seasonings. Add crab meat and mix gently, but thoroughly. If mixture is too dry, add a little more mayonnaise. Shape into 6 cakes. Cook in fry pan, in just enough oil to prevent sticking, until browned on each side (about 5 minutes each side).

Marian Donley, Rincon, GA

"You have heard that it was said, 'Love your neighbor and hate your enemy.' But I tell you: Love your enemies and pray for those who persecute you, that you may be sons of your Father in heaven. He causes his sun to rise on the evil and the good, and sends rain on the righteous and unrighteous. If you love those who love you, what reward will you get? Are not even the tax collectors doing that? And if you greet only your brothers, what are you doing more than others? Do not even pagans do that? Be perfect, therefore, as your heavenly father is perfect.'"

Matthew 5: 43-48

SHRIMP CREOLE

1/2	cup onion, chopped
1/2	cup celery, chopped
1	garlic clove, minced
3	tbsp. oil
1	lb. can tomatoes
1	8 oz. can tomato sauce
1	tsp. salt
1	tsp. sugar
1/2 -1	tsp. chili powder
1	tbsp. worcestershire sauce
3-4	dashes Tabasco sauce
1	tsp. cornstarch
1	lb. raw shrimp, peeled & deveined
1/2	cup green pepper, chopped

Saute onion, celery, and garlic in oil until tender, but not brown. Add tomatoes, tomato sauce, seasonings. Simmer, uncovered for 45 minutes. Mix cornstarch with 2 tsp. water and stir into sauce. Cook and stir until mixture thickens. Add shrimp and green pepper. Cover, simmer until shrimp are done, about 5 minutes. Serve over rice.

Serves 5 to 6

Mariam Hancock, Mulberry St. UMC

"Blessed is the man
who does not walk in the council of the wicked
or stand in the way of sinners
or sit in the seat of mockers.
But his delight is in the law of the Lord,
and on his law he meditates day and night."

Psalm 1: 1-2

The Ten Commandments

I.   You shall have no other Gods before me.

II.   You shall not make for yourself an idol . . .

III.   You shall not misuse the name of the Lord, your God . . .

IV.   Remember the Sabbath day by keeping it holy.

V.   Honor your father and your mother.

VI.   You shall not murder.

VII.   You shall not commit adultery.

VIII.   You shall not steal.

IX.   You shall not give false testimony against your neighbor.

X.   You shall not covet your neighbor's house.

Exodus 20: 1-17

BREADS

"Give us this day, our daily bread..."

Matthew 6:11

CHAPTER FIVE

Jesus often called his disciples together to break bread. After Jesus's death and resurrection, the disciples continued to break bread with one another. Since ancient times man has known the importance of bread as sustainer of life and the importance of sharing life's sustenance in fellowship, one with another.

Jesus called himself the bread of life, comparing himself to the one thing that man required to have life. On the night before his crucifixion broken bread became symbolic of the body of Christ which was about to be broken for us.

And to this very day we celebrate the Lord's Supper and eat bread in remembrance of Him.

Let us break bread together. There's no shortage of selections from which to choose.

"And he took bread, gave thanks and broke it, and gave it to them, saying, 'This is my body given for you; do this in remembrance of me.'
In the same way, after the supper he took the cup saying, 'This cup is the new covenant in my blood, which is poured out for you.'"

Luke 22: 19-20

CORN BREAD

1	pkg. Jiffy corn muffin mix
1/4	cup margarine, melted
1/2	cup milk
1	egg
1	cup whole kernel corn, drained
1	cup mayonnaise
1	onion, chopped
1	cup sour cream
1	cup cheddar cheese, grated
1	tsp. salt

Mix corn muffin mix, margarine, milk and egg. Spread in greased 10x10 baking dish. Mix all other ingredients and spread over cornbread mixture. Top with more grated cheese. Bake in 400 degree oven until done, approximately 40 minutes.

Wednesday Nite Fellowship, First UMC Newnan

JALAPENO CORN BREAD

1 1/2	cup self-rising corn meal
1/4	cup self-rising flour
1	cup buttermilk
2	eggs, beaten
1/2	cup vegetable oil
1	med. onion, chopped
1	8.5 oz. can cream style corn
2 or 3	jalapeno peppers, chopped
1 1/2	cups cheddar cheese, shredded

Preheat oven to 375 degrees. Spray 9x13 baking pan with vegetable cooking spray. Place pan in oven to warm. Mix all ingredients except cheese in large bowl. Pour half of batter into warm prepared pan. Sprinkle half of cheese over batter. Spread remaining batter over mixture and top with rest of cheese. Bake for 35 minutes. Serves 16

Louise Mobley, Jersey UMC

CHEESE WAFERS

1   10 oz. pkg. Cracker Barrel cheese
2   sticks margarine
2   cups flour
2   cups rice krispies
1/2   tsp. salt
       dash of red pepper

Cream together cheese and margarine. Slowly add flour, rice krispies, salt and pepper. Roll into small balls. Mash down with a fork. Bake at 350 degrees for about 15-20 minutes.

Becky Jester, Park Avenue UMC

BISHOP'S BREAD

1 1/2 cup all purpose flour, sifted
1 1/2 tsp. baking powder
1/4   tsp. salt
2/3   cup chocolate chips
2   cups walnuts or pecans, chopped
1   cup dates, finely snipped
1/2   cup halved glazed cherries
3   eggs
1   cup sugar

Preheat oven to 325 degrees. Grease 10x5x3 loaf pan and line bottom with wax paper. Sift flour, baking powder and salt into medium size bowl. Stir in chocolate chips, nuts, dates and cherries. Coat well with flour. Mix eggs with electric mixer and add sugar. Beat well. Fold into flour mixture. Bake 1 1/2 hours or until done. Cool in pan on wire rack. When cool remove from pan. Wrap in foil and store.

Mignon Ridings, First UMC, Smyrna

GRANDMA HANCOCK'S BUTTERMILK BISCUITS

2	cups White Lily all purpose flour, sifted
1	tsp. salt
3	tsp. baking powder
1/2	tsp. soda
3	tbsp. Crisco
1	cup buttermilk

Sift dry ingredients except soda together into bowl. Mix soda with buttermilk. Work (cut) Crisco into flour mixture with pastry blender. Add buttermilk, stirring to make a soft dough. Flour top of dough so that you can handle it. Flour pastry cloth or wax paper lightly. Turn dough onto it. Kneed 5-6 times. Roll to 1/2 to 3/4 inch thickness. Cut out biscuits with a small cookie cutter. Place on greased baking sheet. Bake at 400 degrees until golden.

Whitney & Andrew Hancock, Oak Grove UMC

MONA NESBIT'S SHORTBREAD

1	lb. butter (room temperature)
1	cup powdered sugar
4	cups all purpose flour

Cream together butter and sugar. Add flour one cup at a time. Pat out in jelly roll pan. Prick with fork all over. Bake for 45 minutes in a 325 degree oven. Cut into squares immediately before it hardens.

". . . What is impossible with men is possible with God."

Luke 18: 27

95

HERB BISCUITS

1/2	cup unsalted butter, melted
2	pkgs. of 10 Hungry Jack flaky biscuits
2	tbsp. fresh herbs* or 1 tsp. dried ones

Preheat oven to 375 degrees. Spray entire inside of a bundt pan with vegetable spray. Pour melted butter into pan and sprinkle with herbs. Stand biscuits on edge all around the pan. Bake for 20 to 25 minutes or until golden brown. Turn out onto platter and serve hot. Pull apart to eat.
* Parsley, basil, oregano, thyme, chives, dill, or whatever is available. Mix or use one at a time.

Alice Jo Giddens, Park Ave. UMC

BROCCOLI CORNBREAD

2	boxes Jiffy Corn Muffin Mix
1	medium onion, chopped
1	10 oz. box frozen chopped broccoli, thawed
4	eggs, slightly beaten
1	8 oz. container cottage cheese
1	cup cheese, grated
1 1/2	sticks margarine

Combine all ingredients except margarine. Melt margarine in 9x13 pan and grease well, then pour excess margarine into mixture. Mix batter well. Pour into greased pan. Bake at 375 degrees for about 40-45 minutes

Becky Jester, Park Avenue UMC

EASY ROLLS

6	**cups self-rising flour**
1	**pkg. yeast**
1/2	**cup sugar**
3/4	**cup shortening**
3	**cups lukewarm water**

Sift flour into one bowl. Put yeast, sugar and shortening in a large bowl. Cream well until fluffy. Add flour and water alternately to form a firm dough. Cover bowl; let rise until double in size. Store in refrigerator, covered, until ready to cook. Make out rolls, let rise again until double in size. If rolled out, make about 1/2 inch thickness and cut. If you prefer, you may fill muffin pans 1/2 full and let rise until double in size. Bake at 375 degrees until light brown. Yields 36 medium rolls.

Penny Kilgore, Pomona UMC, Griffin

ANGEL BISCUITS

5	**cups self rising flour**
1/2	**tsp. soda**
2	**pkg. yeast, dissolved in 1/2 cup warm water**
1/4	**cup sugar**
1	**cup Crisco**
2	**cups buttermilk**

Sift and mix dry ingredients thoroughly. Mix (cut) the Crisco into the flour well. Add the remaining ingredients and mix together. Make out into biscuits on floured surface. Use as much dough as needed or refrigerate in covered container for several days. Bake in a 375 to 400 degree oven until golden brown.

Bitzi Potts

BANANA NUT TEA BREAD

2/3	cup Crisco shortening
1 1/3	cups sugar
2	eggs
3	bananas, mashed
2	cups self rising flour
1	cup nuts, chopped

Cream shortening and sugar together. Add eggs. Mash bananas with fork and add to mixture. Add flour. Stir in nuts. Pour into greased and floured loaf pan. Bake at 350 degrees for 30 to 45 minutes. Use a tooth pick to test for doneness. Do not over cook. Will make one large loaf or two smaller ones (adjust cooking time).

Lisa Huckaby

"As the deer pants for streams of water,
so my soul pants for you, O God."

Psalm 42: 1

"I have fought the good fight, I have finished the race,
I have kept the faith. Now there is in store for me
the crown of righteousness, which the Lord, the righteous
judge, will award to me on that day. . ."

2 Timothy 4: 7-8

Love

"If I speak in the tongues of men and angels,
but have not love,
I am only a resounding gong or a clanging cymbal.
If I have the gift of prophesy and can fathom
all mysteries and knowledge,
and if I have a faith that can move mountains,
but have not love,
I am nothing.
If I give all I possess to the poor
and surrender my body to the flames,
but have not love,
I gain nothing.
Love is patient, love is kind.
It does not envy, it does not boast, it is not proud.
It is not rude, it is not self-seeking,
it is not easily angered.
it keeps no record of wrong.
Love never fails. . .
And now these three remain:
faith, hope, and love.
But the greatest of these is love."

I Corinthians 13: 1-8, 13

BEVERAGES

"For John came neither eating nor drinking, and they say, 'He has a demon.' The Son of Man came eating and drinking, and they say, 'Here is a glutton and a drunkard, a friend of tax collectors and sinners.' But wisdom is proved right by her actions."

Matthew 11:18-19

Chapter Six

During the summer of 1998 I had the opportunity to travel with a group of educators to London, England. During our stay our group was treated to a covered dish supper at the church where Georgia's founder, James Edward Oglethorpe, is buried. I was a bit surprised when we were served wine with our meal. Spirits were never a part of the menu at any of the covered dish suppers I had attended.

But sweet tea and lemonade were. They were served in number ten galvanized washtubs, kept cold by block ice. We drank these beverages from Dixie cups. Sometimes we drank tea, sometimes we drank lemonade, and sometimes we mixed them half and half. It's been many, many years since I've seen a washtub filled with tea or lemonade. It's been years since I've seen a washtub at all, for that matter.

Times have changed. People now buy bottles of water at a dollar a shot. Health conscious congregations offer unsweetened ice tea, along with sweet, but for the life of me, I don't understand the point of drinking it. Today's lemonade usually comes from a powdered mix. The time thing, you understand.

In this short chapter I offer a few creative suggestions for tasty beverages and a couple of recipes for washtub iced tea and hand squeezed lemonade. On a hot afternoon in Georgia, they taste much better than the finest wines of Europe.

"Do not tremble, do not be afraid.
Did I not proclaim this and foretell it long ago?
You are my witnesses. Is there any God besides me?
No, there is no other Rock: I know not one."

Isaiah 44: 8

TEA IN A TUB

100	family sized tea bags
5	lbs. sugar
25	gallons of water
1	20 pound block of ice
1	dozen lemons

Bring to a boil five gallons of water. Drop in tea bags. Cover and simmer for thirty minutes. Add sugar and stir until sugar is dissolved. Pour mixture into wash tub, preferably a clean one. Add twenty gallons of water and stir. Cut lemons in half and throw into tub. Just before serving add a twenty pound block of ice. Serve with a dipper into Dixie cups full of crushed ice.

Yields 25 gallons

SWEET ICED TEA

1	gallon water
6	family sized tea bags
4	cups sugar
	lemon slices (optional)

Bring one quart of water to a boil in saucepan. Add tea bags. Turn off heat and steep 10 to 15 minutes. Add sugar and stir to dissolve. Add 3 quarts of water to mixture. Pour into gallon jug and mix well. Write "SWEET" in big letters on a piece of masking tape and attach to the outside of jug before bringing to church dinner. For unsweetened tea (although I can't imagine why anyone would want to drink it that way) follow same recipe and don't add the sugar.

Yields one gallon.

Darrell Huckaby

103

LEMONADE FOR A CROWD

10 12 ounce cans of frozen Lemonade concentrate
1 small bottle lemon juice
12 fresh lemons
4 gallons water

Empty lemonade concentrate into large container. Add lemon juice and water. Stir until mixture is thoroughly dissolved. Cut lemons into slices and add to mixture. Serve over crushed ice.

Yields 5 gallons

Darrell Huckaby

TUB FULL OF DRINKS

1 large washtub (footwashing kind is fine)
30 lbs of ice
dozens of soft drinks of every description

Go to the store one day before the event and have a grand old time buying as many types of soft drinks as you can think of: Coca Colas, Sprites, Seven-ups, Nehi Grape and Orange, Dr. Pepper, Canada Dry Ginger Ale, and Yoo Hoo chocolate drink. Under no circumstances should you buy any bottled water. If it is absolutely necessary to include diet drinks or Pepsi Colas, do so, but only if it is absolutely necessary. Buy at least one drink for every adult you are expecting and two for every child. Double the amount if an all day singing will follow dinner. Place the drinks in a refrigerator over night. Take them out about an hour before serving. Place them in a great big tub and cover with ice. Your bucket of drinks will be the hit of the party.

Yields as many servings as you put in the tub.

CROWD PLEASING PUNCH

1	12 oz. can frozen orange juice
1	6 oz. can frozen lemonade
1	6 oz. can frozen limeade
1	46 oz. can pineapple juice
2	cups strong unsweetened tea
2	cups sugar
1	l liter of ginger ale
	water

Dissolve sugar in hot water. Add sugar mixture and all ingredients except ginger ale into a one gallon container. Add water to make container 3/4 full. Mix well and leave refrigerated overnight. Just before serving, add ginger ale.

Yields 1 gallon

". . . a wedding took place at Cana, in Galilee. Jesus' mother
was there . . . and . . . when the wine was gone,
Jesus' mother said to him, 'They have no more wine.'
'Dear woman, why do you involve me?' Jesus replied.
'My time has not yet come.'
His mother said to the servants, 'Do whatever he says.'
. . . Jesus said to the servants, 'Fill the jars with water,' so
they filled them to the brim. Then he told them, 'Now draw
some out and take it to the master of the banquet.'
. . . and the master of the banquet tasted the water that had
been turned to wine. . . and said, ' Everyone brings out the
choice wine first and then the cheaper wine after the guests
have had too much to drink;
but you saved the best until now.'
This, the first of his miraculous signs, Jesus performed at
Cana in Galilee. He thus revealed his glory, and his disciples
put their faith in him."

John 2: 1-11

105

DESSERTS

"So I commend the enjoyment of life, because nothing is better for a (person) under the sun than to eat, drink, and be glad ..."

Ecclesiastes 8:15

CHAPTER SEVEN

This came to me as an e-mail from a friend. There was no source listed. You know how these things are circulated through cyberspace. My apologies to the original author.

A minister had been summoned to the home of an elderly parishioner. She wanted to discuss her funeral plans with him. To his surprise, she expressed a desire to be buried with her Bible in one hand and her fork in the other.

"A fork?" responded the pastor. "Why in the world do you want to be buried with a fork."

With a twinkle in her eye, the lady explained. "I've been reminiscing lately about all those wonderful covered dish dinners I've attended over the years. I couldn't begin to count them, but at every one, as the dishes were being gathered up, someone would always remind everyone, 'Keep your fork.'

"I always knew what that meant. Dessert

"We weren't talking about a store bought cookie or a cup of Jello, either. I knew we were about to be served somebody's best layer cake, or pecan pie, or some other wonderful dish. People always brought their very best to church dinners.

"I knew that if somebody told me to keep my fork, the best was yet to come!

"That's exactly what I want people to talk about at my funeral. I don't mind if they take some time to remember all the good times we've had together, but I don't want anybody feeling sad for me because I'm gone.

"When the walk past my open casket and see me in my prettiest blue dress I want them to turn and say to one another, 'Why in the world does she have a fork?'

"That's where you come in. When you preach my funeral I want you to tell everybody that I kept my fork, because I was absolutely certain that the best is yet to come!"

APPLESAUCE SPICE CAKE

1/2	cup butter or shortening
1	cup sugar
2	eggs, beaten lightly
1/2	cup nuts, chopped
1	cups raisins, chopped
2	cups cake flour, sifted
1	tsp. baking soda
1/2	tsp. nutmeg
1	tsp. cinnamon
1	cup unsweetened applesauce

Cream shortening and sugar together. Add eggs and mix thoroughly. Add nuts and raisins. Sift dry ingredients together 3 times and add alternately with applesauce to creamed mixture, beating thoroughly after each addition. Pour into a greased loaf pan and bake at 350 degrees for 1 hour.

Mrs. Olin (Runell) Allen, North Covington Methodist Church

"I will lift up mine eyes unto the hills,
from whence cometh my help.
My help cometh from the Lord, which made heaven and earth.
He will not suffer thy foot to be moved:
he that keepeth thee will not slumber.
Behold,
he that keepeth Israel shall neither slumber nor sleep.
The Lord is thy keeper: The Lord is thy shade upon thy right hand.
The sun shall not smite thee by day, nor the moon by night.
The Lord shall preserve thee from all evil:
he shall preserve thy soul.
The Lord shall preserve thy going out and thy coming in
from this time forth, and even for evermore."

Psalm 121

APPLESAUCE CAKE

1 1/4	cup all purpose flour
1	cup sugar
1 1/4	tsp. soda
1 1/4	tsp. salt
1/8	tsp. baking powder
1/2	tsp. ground cinnamon
1/4	tsp. ground cloves
1/4	tsp. ground allsprice
1/4	cup soft shortening
1/4	cup water
3/4	cup applesauce
1	egg
1/4	cup pecans, chopped
1/2	cup raisins

Combine all ingredients in a mixing bowl. Blend for 3 1/2 minutes. Pour into greased and floured 9" loaf pan. Bake at 350 degrees for 60 - 65 minutes.

Cindy Shorb

"It was written in Isaiah the prophet:
'I will send my messenger ahead of you,
who will prepare your way, a voice of one
calling in the dessert,
'Prepare the way for the Lord,
make straight paths for him.'
And so John came, baptizing in the dessert region
and preaching a baptism of repentance for the
forgiveness of sins."

Mark 1: 2-4

RAW APPLE CAKE

1 1/2	cups Crisco oil
4	eggs
2	cups sugar
3	cups all purpose flour
1	tsp. soda
1	tsp. salt
1	cup nuts, chopped
1	cup raisins
1	cup coconut
3	cups raw crisp apples, chopped fine
1	tsp. vanilla flavoring

Soak the raisins in 1 cup boiling water for 30 minutes to tenderize. Beat the oil, eggs, and sugar in a mixer. Add the flour, soda, salt, nuts, raisins, coconut, vanilla flavoring. Bake in a greased and floured tube pan at 350 degrees for 1 hour.

Filling:

1	cup brown sugar
1	stick margarine
1	small can Carnation milk
1	tsp. vanilla

Mix together and boil for 3 minutes. Pour over cake when you take it out of oven. Let it stand in pan until set.

Mary Huckaby Bouchillon, North Covington Methodist Church

"Judge not, and ye shall not be judged:
condemn not, and ye shall not be condemned:
forgive and ye shall be forgiven."

Luke 6: 37

111

APRICOT NECTAR CAKE

1	box yellow cake mix
4	egg yolks, separated
3	tsp. lemon extract
3/4	cups cooking oil
1	cup apricot nectar
1	box lemon Jello

Separate the eggs, putting the egg whites into small mixing bowl. Put the yolks and remaining 5 ingredients into a large mixing bowl and mix until well blended. Beat the egg whites, then fold into the batter. Pour batter into a greased and floured tube pan. Cook at 325 degrees for 45 minutes to 1 hour.

Make a glaze of 1 1/2 cups powdered sugar and juice of 2 lemons or 1/4 cup lemon juice. Blend the glaze and pour over hot cake. If the glaze seems too thin add more powdered sugar gradually until you get the right consistency.

Miss Kathryn R. House RN, North Covington Methodist Church

"Praise the Lord, O my soul;
all my inmost being, praise his holy name.
Praise the Lord, O my soul,
and forget not all his benefits.
He forgives all my sins
and heals all my diseases;
he redeems my life from the pit
and crowns me with love and compassion.
He satisfies my desires with good things,
so that my youth is renewed like the eagle's."

Psalm 103: 1-5

APRICOT NECTAR CAKE #2

1	box lemon supreme cake mix
1	cup apricot nectar
1/2	cup sugar
4	eggs
1	cup vegetable oil
2	tbsp. flour

Mix sugar and eggs. Add oil, cake mix, flour and nectar. Mix well. Pour into a well greased tube (NOT BUNDT) pan. Bake at 350 degrees for 60 minutes. Remove from oven and allow to stand 15 minutes. Remove cake from pan. Make a sauce of 1 cup sifted powdered sugar, 3/4 cup apricot nectar and juice of 1 lemon.

Mix well, then spoon over cake. Allow to soak into cake.

Peg Rosing

"Jesus said, 'A certain man was going down from Jerusalem to Jericho; and he fell among robbers, and they stripped him and beat him, and went off leaving him half dead. And a certain priest was going down on that road, and when he saw him, he passed by on the other side. And a Levite also, when he came to the place and saw him, passed by on the other side. But a certain Samaritan, who was on a journey, came upon him, and when he saw him, he felt compassion . . . Which of these three do you think proved to be a neighbor to the man who was robbed?"

Luke 10: 30-33, 36

BROWN CARAMEL CAKE

1	cup butter
2	cups sugar
3	cups all purpose flour
1	cup milk
4	eggs
2	tsp. baking powder

Cream butter and sugar; add 1 egg at a time and beat well. Add milk, flour and baking powder. Beat until smooth. Put in two 9 inch layer pans and bake at 350 degrees for 30 minutes.
Filling:

3	cups sugar
1/2	cup browned sugar
1 1/2	cup carnation milk
1/2	cup butter

Brown 1/2 cup sugar and place with milk, sugar and butter in a boiler. Cook to soft ball. Beat until cooled and place on cake.

In memory of Mrs. John Mask, North Covington Methodist Church

"I am the good shepherd. The good shepherd lays down his life for the sheep. The hired hand is not the shepherd who owns the sheep. So when he sees the wolf coming, he abandons the sheep and runs away. Then the wolf attacks the flock and scatters it. The man runs away because he is a hired hand and cares nothing for the sheep."

John 10: 11-13

CARROT AND PINEAPPLE CAKE

3	cups all purpose flour
2	cups sugar
2	tsp. baking powder
2	tsp. cinnamon
2	tsp. soda
1	tsp. salt
1 1/3	cups vegetable oil
3	cups carrots, grated
4	large eggs
1	8 oz. can crushed pineapple w/juice
2	tsp. vanilla

Mix dry ingredients, then add all other ingredients. Pour into a large 3 qt. casserole dish. Bake at 350 degrees for approximately 45 minutes. This is a large cake - 1 1/2 times the regular size.

Arnease Moore

"No man can serve two masters:
for either he will hate the one,
and love the other;
or else he will hold to the one,
and despise the other.
Ye cannot serve God and mammon."

Matthew 6: 24

MARBLED GRASSHOPPER CHEESECAKE

1 1/2	cups chocolate cookie crumbs
1/4	cup sugar
3	tbsp. butter or margarine
4	8 oz. pkgs. cream cheese
1	14 oz. can sweetened condensed milk
4	eggs
2	tsp. vanilla extract
2	tbsp. green creme de menthe
3	tbsp. green creme de cacao
2	drops green food coloring, optional

Preheat oven to 300 degrees. Combine crumbs, sugar, and butter in bowl. Press firmly on bottom of 9 inch spring form pan. In large bowl with electric mixer at medium speed, beat cream cheese until fluffy. Gradually beat in milk until smooth. Add eggs and vanilla; mixing well. Measure 1 1/2 cup batter into medium bowl. Add creme de menthe, creme de cacao and food coloring; mixing well. Pour half the plain batter into prepared pan, then half the flavored batter; repeat. Swirl knife through batters to marbleize. Bake 60 to 70 minutes or until center is set. Cool in pan or wire rack. Refrigerate 2 hours until chilled.

Ellen, Jersey UMC

"But the people who trust the Lord will become strong again.
They will rise up as an eagle in the sky;
they will run and not need rest;
they will walk and not become tired."

Isaiah 41: 31

CHOCOLATE DREAM CAKE

1/2	cup butter or margarine, softened
4	oz. cream cheese, softened
2	cups granulated sugar
2	eggs. slightly beatened
2	tsp. vanilla
2	cups all purpose flour
3/4	cup cocoa
1 1/2	tsp. baking soda
1/2	tsp. salt
1	cup boiling water

Cream butter, cream cheese and sugar until fluffy. Beat in eggs and vanilla. In separate bowl, combine dry ingredients; blend into butter mixture; stir in boiling water. Bake in layers at 350 degrees for 25 to 30 minutes.

Frosting:

2	cups semi-sweet chocolate chips, melted and cooled
1 1/2	cups sour cream
1	tsp. vanilla

Beat ingredients together until smooth. Frost cake.

Mrs. Betty Wood, Sandy Cross UMC, Crawfordville Charge

**"When the day of Pentecost came, they were all
together in one place. Suddenly, a noise like
a strong , blowing wind came down from heaven
and filled the whole house where they were sitting. . .
They were all filled with the Holy Spirit . . ."**

Acts 2: 1-2, 3

Cake Mix Chocolate Cake

1	yellow cake mix
1	cup sour cream
4	eggs
1/2	cup oil
1	small pkg. instant chocolate pudding (dry)
1	large pkg. chocolate chips

Mix and pour into greased Bundt pan. Bake at 350 degrees for 45 to 50 minutes. Cool. Remove from pan and drizzle with fudge sauce.

Alice Jo Giddens, Park Avenue UMC

Chocolate Sheet Cake

1	stick margarine
1/2	cup Crisco
4	tbsp. cocoa
1	cup water
2	cups plain flour
2	cups sugar
1/2	cup buttermilk
2	eggs, beaten
1	tsp. soda
1	tsp. vanilla

Combine margarine, Crisco, cocoa, and water in saucepan. Bring to boil and quickly pour over flour and sugar. Add buttermilk, eggs, soda and vanilla. Mix well and pour into well greased 11x16 pan. Bake at 400 degrees for 20 minutes.

Icing: Ten minutes after cake starts cooking, start icing. Use saucepan and add 1 stick margarine, 4 tbsp. cocoa, 6 tbsp. sweet milk. Bring to boil. Remove from stove and add 1 box 4X sugar, 1 tsp. vanilla, and 1 cup nuts. Beat well and pour over cake immediately. Cool

Mary Akin, Ebenezer UMC

118

HAWAIIAN DREAM CAKE

2   cups plain flour
1   cup self rising flour
2   cups sugar
1   tsp. cinnamon
3   eggs
1   cup vegetable oil
2   tsp. vanilla
1   8 oz. can crushed pineapple w/juice
1   large banana, mashed
1   cup pecans or walnuts

Preheat oven to 300 degrees. Blend dry ingredients by hand. Add other ingredients. Pour into greased and floured tube pan. Bake 50 minutes or until done. Frost with: 3/4 c. sugar, 1/2 cup milk, 3/4 stick margarine, 1 cup flaked coconut, 1/2 cup pecans or walnuts, and 1 tsp. vanilla. Boil all together for 2 minutes. Pour over warm cake.

Dorothy Parker, Jersey UMC

ICE CREAM CAKE

25-30 Oreo cookies
1/2   cup margarine, melted
1/2   gallon vanilla ice cream
        chocolate syrup*
1   large container Cool Whip

Grind cookies. Mix with margarine. Press into 9x13 pan. Freeze. Soften ice cream. Press on top of cookie layer. Freeze. Cover ice cream layer with cooled chocolate syrup. Last top with Cool Whip to form 4th layer. *Syrup recipe: 1 heaping tbsp. cocoa, 2/3 cup milk, 1/2 cup nuts, 1/2 cup margarine, 1 tsp. vanilla, 2/3 cup sugar, pinch of salt. Boil for 4 minutes. Cool before placing on ice cream
layer.

Dorothy Parker, Jersey UMC

JAPANESE FRUIT CAKE

1	cup milk
1	cup butter
2	cups sugar
3	cups self rising flour
5	eggs
1	cup nuts, chopped
1	cup raisins, chopped
1/2	tsp. each of nutmeg, cinnamon, cloves, and allspice

Mix all ingredients together. Pour into 4 greased and floured cake pans. Bake at 325 degrees until done.

Filling: Rind and juice of 1 lemon, juice of 1 orange, milk from 1 coconut, the grated coconut, 2 cups sugar, 1 tbsp. flour, butter the size of a walnut. Cook until it will spread on the layers.

In memory of Mrs. A. L. Huckaby, North Covington Methodist Church

GRANNY AVARY'S POUND CAKE

3	cups plain flour
3	cups sugar
9	eggs
1 1/2	cups shortening
1 1/2	tsp. lemon or vanilla extract

Combine all ingredients in a large mixing bowl. Blend until smooth. Beat at medium speed with electric mixer for 15 minutes or until very fluffy. Pour into a greased and floured 10 inch tube pan. Bake at 300 degrees for 1 hour, 25 minutes. Remove from pan. Cool on wire rack.

Mary Akin, Ebenezer UMC

KAY'S POUND CAKE

1	cup Crisco
3	cups sugar
3	cups all purpose flour
6	eggs
1	tsp. lemon flavoring
1	tsp. butter & nut flavoring
1	8 oz. Cool Whip

Cream sugar and Crisco. Add eggs one at a time. Add flour. Fold in Cool Whip. Bake at 325 degrees for 1 hour and 15 minutes. (This cake is very moist!)

Peggy Price, Hartwell, GA

POUND CAKE

1/2	cup butter
1/2	cup Crisco
2 3/4	cups sugar
3	cups plain flour
1/2	tsp. baking powder
1	cup sweet milk
5	eggs
1	tsp. vanilla flavoring

Cream butter, Crisco and sugar together. Add eggs. Beat until smooth.. Sift the baking powder with the flour. Add flour mixture and milk alternately to the butter mixture. Add vanilla. Pour into a greased and floured tube pan. Cook at 325 degrees for 1 hour and 15 minutes.

Mrs. D.W. (Myrtle) House, North Covington Methodist Church

121

POUND CAKE #2

1	lb. shortening (I use 1/2 butter & 1/2 Crisco)
3	cups sugar
4	cups plain flour
10	medium eggs
1	tsp. butter flavoring
1/2	tsp. vanilla
1/2	tsp. lemon flavoring

Sift flour 3 times and measure. Sift flour and sugar together. Cream butter or shortening well. Add sugar and flour mixture. Add 1 egg at a time, beating after each addition. Add flavoring. Pour into a floured 10 inch tube pan. Bake at 300 degrees about 2 hours or until done. Start in cold oven.

Margaret Albright, Carrollton First UMC

CHOCOLATE POUND CAKE

3	cups plain flour
3	cups sugar
1/2	cup cocoa
1 1/2	cups sweet milk
6	eggs
2	sticks margarine
1/2	cup Crisco
1	tsp. vanilla
1	tsp. salt
1	tsp. baking powder

Mix all ingredients. Bake in a tube pan at 325 degrees for 1 1/2 hours.

Filling: 2 cups sugar, 1/4 cup cocoa, 2/3 cups milk, and 1 stick margarine. Boil for 3 minutes and let cool. Beat and spread on cake.

In memory of Mrs. T.A. McCrary, North Covington Methodist Church

CHOCOLATE POUND CAKE #2

1/2	lb. butter
1/2	cup vegetable shortening
3	cups sugar
1/4	tsp. salt
1/2	cup cocoa
1 1/4	cups sweet milk
5	eggs
2/3	tsp. baking powder
3	cups plain flour
1	tsp. vanilla

Sift dry ingredients together. Cream butter, shortening, and sugar. Add other ingredients and cook at 300 degrees for 1 hour and 25 minutes. Icing: 1/2 cup cocoa, 1 box 4x sugar, 8 tbsp. undiluted evaporated milk, 1 stick margarine, 1 tsp. vanilla. Bring butter and milk to a boil, stirring. Take off stove and add sifted sugar and cocoa. Beat until smooth.

Mrs. Don (Mary) Ballard, North Covington Methodist Church

COCONUT POUND CAKE

3	sticks margarine
3	cups sugar
6	eggs
1	can coconut
1	cup milk
3	cups plain flour
1	tsp. baking powder
1/4	tsp. salt
1	tbsp. lemon flavoring

Cream margarine and sugar together. Add eggs, one at a time. Then add dry ingredients, mixing coconut and lemon flavoring. Pour in tube pan and bake at 350 degrees for 1 hour.

In memory of Mrs. Allie B. Savage, North Covington Methodist Church

CREAM CHEESE POUND CAKE

3	sticks butter
1	8 oz. pkg. cream cheese
3	cups sugar
3	cups cake flour
6	eggs
1	tsp. vanilla
	dash of salt

Cream butter, cream cheese, and sugar until soft and fluffy. Add cake flour and eggs alternately. Add vanilla and salt. Bake in floured and greased tube pan at 350 degrees for 1 hour to 1 1/2 hours.

Anita Baggett, Jersey UMC

MOM'S SOUR CREAM POUND CAKE

2	sticks salted butter
3	cups sugar
1	8 oz. sour cream
1/4	tsp. soda
1	tsp. salt
1	tsp. vanilla
1	tsp. lemon flavoring
3	cups plain flour
6	eggs

Cream butter and sugar well. Add sour cream and soda. Beat well. Add flavorings. Add eggs 2 at a time alternately with 1 cup flour. Beat well after each addition. Cook in tube pan at 350 degrees for 1 hour and 15 minutes. Cool cake on wire rack. (The success of this cake is beating long enough. Have eggs and butter at room temperature before mixing.)

Mary Akin, Ebenezer UMC

CRUSHED PINEAPPLE CAKE

1   pkg. yellow cake mix
1   20 oz. can crushed pineapple
1   cup sugar
1   6 oz, pkg. instant vanilla pudding mix
1   8 oz. container Cool Whip

Prepare cake and bake in a 13 x 9 pan according to package directions. Combine pineapple and sugar in sauce pan and bring to a boil. Cool slightly. When cake is done, remove from oven. Poke holes in cake with a fork. Pour pineapple mixture over top of cake. Set aside to cool. Prepare pudding according to package directions and spread over top of cake. Spread Cool Whip over top of pudding and refrigerate.

Susan Shepard, Jersey UMC

PLAIN CAKE

1   cup Crisco
2   cups sugar
3   cups cake flour
2   tsp. baking powder
1/4   tsp. salt
4   eggs
1   cup sweet milk
1/2   tsp. vanilla flavoring
1/2   tsp. lemon extract
       few drops almond extract

Cream Crisco and sugar. Sift flour once. Measure 3 cups with baking powder and salt added. Add milk with extracts alternately with dry ingredients. Add eggs, one at a time. Bake in tube pan at 350 degrees in middle of oven for 45 minutes.

In memory of Mrs. I.T. Wiley, North Covington Methodist Church

PLUM NUTTY CAKE

2	cups sugar
1	cup wesson oil
3	eggs, beaten
1	tsp. cinnamon
1	tsp. cloves or nutmeg
2	cups self rising flour, sifted
2	jars plum baby food
1	cup nuts, chopped

Do not beat. Stir ingredients in order as listed in recipe. Pour into a greased and wax paper lined tube pan. Bake at 350 degrees for 1 hour.

Caramel Icing:

1 1/2	cup white sugar
1	cup brown sugar
2/3	cup canned milk
1	stick margarine.

Mix ingredients in a sauce pan and cook for 5 minutes, stirring constantly. Icing is done when soft ball is formed in cold water. Cool icing, then beat until thick enough to spread on cake layers..

Alice Gauntt, Jersey UMC

"Greater love has no one than this,
that one lay down his life for his friends."

John 15: 13

PUMPKIN CAKE

2	cups plain flour
2	tsp. baking powder
2	tsp. soda
2	tsp. cinnamon
1/2	tsp. salt
4	eggs, well beaten
2	cups sugar
1	cup vegetable oil
1	lb. can pumpkin

Sift flour, baking powder, soda, cinnamon, and salt together in small bowl. Beat by hand in a large bowl the eggs and sugar. Add oil and beat well. Add flour mixture and pumpkin, blending well. Pour into tube or bundt pan at 350 degrees for 1 hour and 15 minutes.

Icing:

1	stick softened margarine
8	oz. softened cream cheese
1	box powdered sugar
1	tsp. vanilla

Mix well; spread on cooled cake.

Linda Mitchell, Crawfordville UMC

". . . 'I am the way, and the truth, and the life;
no one comes to the Father, but through Me.' "

John 14: 6

SCOTCH CAKE

2	cups plain flour
2	cups sugar
1	cup margarine
1	cup water
1/3	cup cocoa
2	eggs
1/2	cup buttermilk
1	tsp. soda
1	tsp. cinnamon
1	tsp. vanilla

Mix dry ingredients. Add liquids. Pour into well greased 9x13 pan. Bake at 350 degrees for 30 minutes. Icing: 1/2 cup margarine, 1/4 cup cocoa, 6 tbsp. milk and 1 box powdered sugar. Mix all ingredients and spread on cool cake.

Wednesday Night Fellowship, First UMC Newnan

TURTLE CAKE

1	box German chocolate cake mix
1	stick margarine
1	6 oz. pkg. chocolate chips
1	pkg. lite caramels
1	can sweetened condensed milk
1	cup walnuts, chopped

Prepare cake mix as directed on box. Pour 1/2 batter into greased and floured cake pan. Bake at 350 degrees for 15 minutes. Cool. Melt caramels, margarine and milk until thick and creamy. Pour caramel mixture over cooked cake. Sprinkle with chocolate chips and walnuts. Pour remaining batter on top. Bake at 350 degrees for 25 minutes more.

Mary Ann Holder, Ebenezer UMC

CARAMEL FROSTING

1 1/2	cup white sugar
1/2	cup brown sugar
2/3	cup evaporated or whole milk
1	stick margarine

Combine all ingredients in heavy saucepan. Gradually bring to boil, stirring until sugar is dissolved. Boil until mixture reaches the soft ball stage. Remove from heat, beat until right consistency to spread on cool cake. Ices a 2 layer cake.

Frances McKissick, Jersey UMC

NEVER FAIR CHOCOLATE ICING

1/3	cup milk
1	cup sugar
5	tsp. margarine
1	6 oz. pkg. chocolate chips

Bring first 3 ingredients to boil. Boil 1 minute. Add chocolate chips and beat until smooth. Can be put on warm or cold cake. Will ice a 2 layer or 1 sheet cake.

Jane Lyle, Ebenezer UMC

"A new commandment I give to you,
that you love one another,
even as I have loved you,
that you also love one another."

John 13: 34

CHOCOLATE ICING

2 1/2	cups sugar
1	cup canned milk
1/4	cup cocoa
2	tbsp. white Karo syrup
1	stick margarine
1	tsp. vanilla

Cook for about 4 minutes until a soft ball forms in cold water. Add vanilla and beat until it will spread on cake.

In memory of Mrs. A. L. Huckaby, North Covington Methodist Church

FUDGE

1	stick margarine
2	cups sugar
10	large marshmallows
3/4	cup evaporated milk
1 1/2	cups chocolate chips
1	cup nuts, chopped
2	tsp. vanilla

Melt margarine. Add marshmallows and melt. Add sugar and milk. Bring to a boil and cook for exactly 6 minutes, stirring constantly. Add chocolate chips, nuts and vanilla. Stir rapidly. Pour into buttered 8" square dish. Can make butterscotch candy by using the butterscotch chips instead of chocolate.

Virginia Wray, Ebenezer UMC

MICROWAVE PEANUT BRITTLE

1	cup raw peanuts
1	cup sugar
1/2	cup light corn syrup
1/8	tsp. salt
1	tsp. butter
1	tsp. vanilla
1	tsp. soda

Combine first 4 ingredients in 1 1/2 qt. pyrex bowl. Microwave on high for 4 minutes. Stir. Cook 4 more minutes. Stir in butter and vanilla. Cook 1 minute. Remove from microwave. Rapidly stir in 1 tsp. soda. Quickly pour mixture onto greased cookie sheet. Cool and break into pieces.

Jackie Batchelor, Jersey UMC

PRALINES

1	lb. light brown sugar
2	cups granulated sugar
1	cup whipping cream
1/2	tsp. salt
4	tbsp. real butter
1	lb. pecan halves

Combine first four ingredients in large heavy pot. Stir continually over medium heat until candy thermometer reads 228 degrees F. Add butter and pecan halves. Stir until thermometer reaches 238 degrees. Cool until mixture thickens, stirring regularly. Beat with wooden spoon until gloss reduced. Drop on greased aluminum
foil by spoonful in praline shape. Cool until completely firm. These make wonderful Christmas presents in jars or boxes.

Arnease Moore

JACKIE'S ROCKY CANDY

1	12 oz. milk chocolate chips
2	cups miniature marshmallows
1	cup nuts, broken

Place chocolate chips in medium size pyrex bowl. Microwave on high for 2 minutes. Stir after first minute. After second minute, stir in marshmallows and nuts. Spread onto cookie sheet lined with wax paper. Refrigerate until firm. Break into bite size pieces.

Lucy Barrett, Jersey UMC

PECAN PIE

1	cup Karo syrup
1/2	cup sugar
1/4	cup margarine, melted
3	eggs, beaten
1/4	tsp. salt
1	tsp. vanilla
1	cup pecans
1	unbaked pie shell

Mix eggs, sugar, syrup, salt, vanilla, and margarine. Spread pecans in bottom of pie shell. Pour in filling. Bake at 350 degrees for 30 to 45 minutes or until knife blade inserted comes out clean.

Mary Akin, Ebenezer UMC

"Let not your heart be troubled:
believe in God, believe also in Me."

John 14: 1

EASY CHOCOLATE CHIP COOKIES

1	box butter recipe cake mix
1/2	cup all purpose flour
2/3	cup oil (or applesauce)
2	eggs
1	cup chocolate chips
1	cup pecans/walnuts, finely chopped

Mix all ingredients well. Bake on ungreased baking sheet at 350 degrees for 12 minutes or until done.

Arnease Moore

MEMORY BOOK COOKIES

1	cup margarine, softened
2	cups brown sugar (firmly packed)
2	large eggs
1	tsp. vanilla
3 1/2	cups plain flour
1	tsp. baking soda
1/2	tsp. salt
1	cup pecans

Cream margarine and brown sugar; beat well. Add eggs and vanilla; mix well. Add dry ingredients; mix well. Add pecans. Roll and wrap in waxed paper. Chill 4 hours. Slice and bake at 350 degrees for 10-12 minutes.

Linda Mitchell, Crawfordwille UMC

KATHRYN'S BAKED MERINGUES

1   egg white
1/2   tsp. vanilla flavoring
1/2   cup light brown sugar (packed)
2   cups pecans, (halves & quarters)

Beat egg white until stiff; add vanilla, beat a little more. Add sugar and beat until real thick. Add pecans, coat real well, then drop by teaspoonsful on greased cookie sheet. Bake at 250 degrees until good and firm. They will be cracked on top. Time will be approximately 1 hour. When done, turn stove off and leave meringues until completely cold.

Kathryn R. House RN, North Covington Methodist Church

SIS'S SUGAR COOKIES

4   cups unsifted all purpose flour
1   tsp. salt
1   tsp. baking soda
1   tsp. cream of tartar
1   cup butter or margarine
1   cup vegetable oil
1   cup confectioner's sugar
1   cup granulated sugar
2   eggs
1   tsp. vanilla extract

In medium bowl, combine flour, salt, baking soda, and cream of tartar. In large mixer at medium speed, cream butter, oil, confectioner's sugar and 1 cup of granulated sugar until light and fluffy. Add eggs and vanilla and continue beating, scraping sides of bowl. Gradually add dry ingredients; mix until just combined. Wrap and refrigerate dough at least one hour. Shape dough into 1 inch balls; roll in additional sugar. Place on greased cookie sheets. Press each ball with a fork. Bake at 350 degrees for 10 to 12 minutes. Remove immediately to wire racks to cool. Makes 8-10 dozen.

Alice Jo Giddens, Park Avenue UMC

TEA CAKES

1	stick butter
1	cup sugar
1	egg
2	cups self rising flour
1	tsp. vanilla flavoring

Mix sugar and butter by hand. Add egg, flour, and vanilla. Roll out real thin. Bake at 350 degrees until slightly brown. Dough handles better if cold.

In memory of Mrs. A.L. Huckaby, North Covington Methodist Church

APPLESAUCE CASSEROLE

2	cups applesauce
1	stick margarine, melted
1	cup milk
3/4	cup sugar
2	eggs
1	cup vanilla wafers, crushed

Beat eggs, add sugar, milk and margarine. Stir in vanilla wafers and applesauce. Mix well. Bake in a deep dish casserole at 350 degrees for 1 hour. Great as a side dish or served cold with ice cream!

Torri Frank, Ebenezer UMC

**"I will sing of the mercies of the Lord forever;
with my mouth I will make known thy faithfulness
to all generations."**

Psalm 89: 1

BROWNIES

4	oz. unsweetened chocolate
2/3	cup shortening
2	cups sugar
4	eggs
1	tsp. vanilla
1 1/4	cup self rising flour
1	cup nuts, chopped

Melt chocolate and shortening in large saucepan over low heat. Remove from heat. Mix in sugar, eggs and vanilla. Stir in remaining ingredients. Spread in 9x13x2 greased baking pan. Bake at 350 degrees for 30 minutes or until brownies start to pull away from sides of pan. Do not overbake. Cool slightly. Cut into bars. If desired, spread with glossy chocolate frosting.

Susan Ballard, North Covington Methodist Church

DIRT DESSERT

2	boxes (9 oz. each) chocolate wafers
1/2	stick margarine
1	8 oz. pkg. cream cheese
1	cup powdered sugar
2	small boxes instant vanilla pudding
3 1/2	cups milk
1	12 oz. container Cool Whip

Crush wafers in food processor to a fine texture. Set aside. Cream together margarine, cream cheese and powdered sugar. Set aside. Mix pudding with milk. Fold in Cool Whip. Add creamed mixture to pudding mixture. Mix well Alternate layers of crushed wafers and cream mixture in bowl, starting and ending with wafers. Refrigerate.

Chris Hiner

REFRIGERATED FIX AHEAD DESSERT

1   angel food cake
1   8 oz. cartons strawberry yogurt
2   pts. strawberries, frozen, cut up (not whole)
1   8 oz. carton Cool Whip

Crumble up (not too small) angel food cake in deep glass dish. (Truffle is pretty!) Layer in order: cake, yogurt, strawberries, Cool Whip. Repeat. Top layer should be Cool Whip. Cover with plastic wrap. May be made days ahead.

Jane Lyle, Ebenezer UMC

JELLO FINGERS

3   3 oz pkg. Jello, any flavor
4   envelopes unflavored gelatin
4   cups boiling water

Mix all together. Pour into 9x13 inch pan. Chill. Cut into cubes. You can put in children's lunches. Refrigeration not required.

Rebecca Hunter, North Covington Methodist Church

"And my people, who are called by my name
humble themselves and pray, and seek my face
and turn from their wicked ways, then I will
hear from heaven, will forgive their sin,
and heal their land."

2 Chronicles 7: 14

A TRIFLE DIFFERENT DESSERT

1	8 oz. vanilla yogurt
2	large boxes sugar free vanilla instant pudding
1	loaf low fat or fat free pound cake
1	cup all fruit strawberry preserves
1	cup fresh strawberries, sliced
1	cup fresh bananas, sliced
2	tbsp. walnuts, chopped
2	tbsp. chocolate cookie crumbs or sprinkles
	lite whipped topping
	whole strawberries

The day before place the yogurt in cheesecloth over a bowl. Allow to drain in the refrigerator overnight until much of the liquid drains out. Prepare instant pudding using 1% or skim milk. (Use a little less milk than called for on the package.). Set aside. Using a deep glass bowl (allowing a view of the beautiful layers), place a layer of thickly sliced pound cake along the bottom. Spread with strawberry preserves. Add a layer of vanilla pudding. Cover the pudding layer with sliced strawberries and bananas. Place a layer of thickened yogurt on top of this. Depending on the bowl size and if there is a sufficient amount of ingredients remaining, repeat layers. Cool in refrigerator for 1 1/2 hour. Spoon whipped topping over top. Sprinkle with chopped walnuts and cookie crumbs. Garnish with whole strawberries.

Carrie Wray

"I can do all things through Christ, who strengthens me."

Philippians 4: 13

PECAN SURPRISES

6   **egg whites,**
2   **cups sugar**
1   **stack Ritz crackers, crushed**
1   **tsp. vanilla**
2   **cups pecans, chopped**

Beat eggs whites, add sugar, mixing well. Add crackers, vanilla, and pecans. Spread into a 9x13 pan. Bake at 350 degrees for 20 minutes or until lightly brown.
Let cool and spread Cool Whip on top. Delicious and easy to make.

Edith C. Sanders, Hartwell, GA

PLAZA PARK SQUARES

1   **box butter cake mix**
1   **stick margarine, softened**
1   **cup pecans, chopped**
1   **egg**
1   **8 oz. pkg. cream cheese, softened**
1   **box confectioner's sugar**
2   **eggs**

Combine cake mix, margarine, pecans and 1 egg by hand. Press into a well greased 9x13 pan. Mix cream cheese, sugar and 2 eggs until well blended. Pour over cake and bake at 350 degrees for 35-40 minutes. Cool and cut into small squares. (Use a sharp knife for cutting. Dip in water between cuts to prevent cake from sticking to knife.)

Virginia Wray

GRANDMA'S GRATED SWEET POTATO PUDDING

4	medium sweet potatoes, grated
2	cups sugar
1/4	cup karo syrup
1	cup butter, melted
4	eggs
2	cups sweet milk
1	cup coconut, grated
3/4	cup raisins
1	cup walnuts or pecan, chopped
1/4	tsp. cinnamon and allspice

Beat eggs, add sugar and butter. Fold in all other ingredients. Mix well. Cook 1 1/2 hours at 300 degrees. Serve with whipped cream.

Nan Curry, Trinity UMC, LaGrange

APPLE CRUMBLE PIE

4	cups apples, sliced
1/2	cup water
3/4	cup sugar
3/4	cups flour
1	stick margarine

Place apples and water in greased pan or dish. Crumble sugar, flour and margarine with fork. Spread over apples. Cook at 350 degrees for 30 minutes.

In memory of Mrs.Ben House, North Covington Methodist Church

BUTTERSCOTCH PIE

2	cups milk
1	cup brown sugar
3	egg yolks, reserving whites for meringue
2	heaping tbsp. cornstarch
	pinch salt
1	tsp. vanilla
2	tbsp. butter
1	9" baked pie shell

Put milk in saucepan on medium heat. Add brown sugar and egg yolks. Put enough water in cornstarch to make paste. Add to sauce pan. Stir until thick. Add vanilla and butter. Stir and pour in 9" baked pie shell. Make meringue with 3 egg whites and sugar.

Julia L. Reed, Asbury UMC, Janesville, WI

SPRING BREEZE CHEESE PIE

1	8 oz. pkg. cream cheese, softened
1/3	cup sugar
1	cup sour cream
2	tsp. vanilla
1	8 oz. carton Cool Whip, thawed
1	graham cracker pie shell
	fresh berries for garnish

Beat cheese until smooth, gradually beating in sugar. Blend in sour cream and vanilla. Fold in Cool Whip and blend well. Spoon into pie shell and chill at least 4 hours. Garnish with any fresh fruit or berries that you may desire.

Wanda Parrish, Rincon, GA

CHESS PIE

1	cup brown sugar, firmly packed
1/2	cup white sugar
1	tbsp. flour
2	eggs
2	tbsp. sweet milk
1/2	cup butter, melted
1	tsp. vanilla

Mix sugar and flour thoroughly. Beat in eggs, milk, butter and vanilla. Mix well. Pour into unbaked pie shell. Bake at 300 degrees for 45 minutes or until firm.

In memory of Mrs. Zed Steel, North Covington Methodist Church

CHOCOLATE PIE

2	cups sweet milk
1	cup sugar
1/3	cup constarch
3	egg yolks (reserve whites for meringue)
1/2	tsp. salt
1	tsp. vanilla
2	tbsp. butter
1	heaping tbsp. cocoa
3	egg whites
6	tbsp. sugar
1/4	tsp. baking powder

Scald milk in double boiler. Mix sugar, cornstarch, egg yolks, salt and cocoa. Add to milk and cook stirring constantly until thick. Cool and add flavoring. Pour into baked pie shell and cover with meringue made with stiffly beaten egg whites, sugar and baking powder.. Cook pie shell at 475 degrees for 10 to 12 minutes. Cook pie at 375 degrees for 12 to 15 minutes.

Margaret Albright, Carrollton First UMC

JACKIE'S PEACH COBBLER

1/4	cup butter or margarine
1	cup self rising flour
2/3	cup sugar
1/4	tsp. cinnamon
1/4	tsp. nutmeg
2/3	cup milk
1	29 oz. can sliced peaches, undrained

Melt butter in 2 quart baking dish or pan. Combine flour, sugar, spices with milk, Pour over melted butter. Do not stir. Add fruit and juice. Do not stir. Bake 40 to 45 minutes at 375 degrees or until crust rises and browns.

Luce Barrett, Jersey UMC.

COBBLER PIE

3/4	cup flour
1	cup sugar
3/4	cup milk
2	tsp. baking powder
1	stick butter
	pinch of salt

Place stick of butter in casserole dish or pan. Mix flour, sugar, baking powder and salt together. Add milk and stir until well mixed. Pour into casserole over melted butter. Then pour large can peaches in middle of this and cook in oven at 350 degrees for 45 minutes or until brown.

In memory of Mrs. Thelma Geiger, North Covington Methodist Church

143

Coconut Pie

1 1/2	cups flake coconut
3	eggs
1/4	cup buttermilk
1 1/4	cups sugar
1	tsp. vanilla
1/2	stick margarine, softened

Beat eggs lightly. Add sugar, margarine, buttermilk and vanilla. Mix well. Stir in coconut and pour into unbaked pie shell. Bake at 375 degrees for 10 minutes. Lower temperature to 300 degrees and bake until golden brown.

Frances Edwards, Ebenezer UMC

Coconut Pie #2

1 1/2	cup grated coconut
3	eggs
1/3	cup buttermilk
1 1/4	cup sugar
1	tsp. vanilla
3/4	stick margarine, melted

Beat eggs slightly. Add sugar, melted margarine, buttermilk, flavoring and coconut. Mix well and pour into unbaked pie shell. Bake at 375 degrees for 10 minutes. Lower oven to 300 degrees and bake until golden brown.

Frances McKissick, Jersey UMC

Peach Custard Pie

1	11 oz. box dried peaches
6	egg yolks (reserve whites for meringue)
2	whole eggs
1/2	cup milk
1/2	cup sugar
1 1/2	cup sugar

Place peaches in sauce pan; cover with water to about 2 inches above peaches. Bring o boil; turn heat down and let simmer until all water is gone, stirring often. (A small amount of water may need to be added to cook peaches completely done.) Add 1 1/2 cups sugar to peaches and mix well; pour into two pie shells.

Mix all eggs, milk, and 1/2 cup sugar together and pour over peaches in pie shells; dot with butter. Bake at 350 degrees for 30 minutes, then lower oven to 300 degrees and bake for 1 more hour.

Meringue: Beat 6 egg whites until stiff, add 6 tbsp. sugar gradually. Add vanilla and beat 2 more minutes. Pile on top of pies and return to 300 degree oven until lightly browned.

Emily R. Barwick, Sandy Cross UMC, Crawfordville Charge

Fresh Strawberry Pie

2	cups water
1 1/2	cups sugar
1/4	cup cornstarch or 1/2 cup flour
1	3 oz. pkg. strawberry Jello
2	pt. fresh strawberries

Mix sugar and cornstarch. Add water and bring to a boil for 3 minutes. Add Jello. Cool and add washed and capped fresh strawberries. Pour into two baked and cooled pie shells. You can also use this recipe with black cherry flavored gelatin and blueberries.

Mrs. Don (Mary) Ballard, North Covington Methodist Church

CREAMY LEMON PIE

1 3/4　cups cold milk
2　　　pks. (4 serving size) Jello vanilla instant pudding
1　　　can (6 oz.) frozen lemonade (thawed)
1　　　8 oz. bowl Cool Whip
1　　　prepared graham cracker crust

Pour milk into large bowl, add pudding mixes. Beat with whisk 30 seconds. add lemonade, beat 30 seconds. (mixture will be thick.) Immediately stir in Cool Whip, Spoon into crust. Refrigerate 4 hours or until set. Garnish with lemon slices if desired. Store leftover pie in the refrigerator. Makes 8 servings.

Edith Sanders, Hartwell, Georgia

CREAM CHEESE SQUARES

1　　　box yellow cake mix
1　　　stick butter or margarine, melted
4　　　eggs
1　　　8 oz. pkg. cream cheese, softened
1　　　box 10x powdered sugar

Mix dry cake mix, melted butter, and 1 beaten egg. Press into bottom of ungreased 9x 13 pyrex cake dish.
Soften the cream cheese. Add 3 beaten eggs and powdered sugar. Mix until smooth.
Pour over first mixture and bake at 350 for 45 minutes or until golden brown and glossy on top.
Cool and cut into squares.
(sometimes I place chocolate chips over the layer and pour the cream cheese mixture over the top. It would probably be good with nuts or butterscotch morsels too!)

Eloise Gerecitano, First United Methodist Church of Tucker

FRENCH COCONUT PIE

3	eggs
1	cup sugar
3/4	stick margarine, melted
1/4	cup buttermilk
1	tsp vanilla
1	3 1/4 oz. can coconut
1	frozen pie crust

Beat eggs slightly. Add sugar, margarine, vanilla, and buttermilk. Stir in coconut. Mix well and pour into unbaked pie crust. Bake at 375 degrees for 10 minutes. Lower heat to 300 degrees and bake until golden brown.

Mrs. Ed. (Dot) Hooten, North Covington UMC

NO CRUST EGG CUSTARD PIE

1	cup sugar
1	tbsp. margarine
1	tbsp. vanilla
3	eggs
2	tbsp. self-rising flour
1	large can evaporated milk

Mix margarine, sugar, and eggs, beating after each addition. Add flour, milk, and vanilla. Pour into greased pie pan and bake at 350 degrees for 30 to 40 minutes until set.

Jackie Batchelor, Jersey UMC

LAUGHTER, THE BEST MEDICINE

"A cheerful heart is good medicine, but a downcast spirit dries up the bones."

Proverbs 17:22

Chapter Eight

If we can't laugh and be happy in church, where in the world can we laugh and be happy? Let's face it. Sometimes funny things happen in church. The spontaneous events are usually the funniest. Of course, most preachers, have a large collection of funny stories. Some of them may even be true. If they aren't, well a very wise man, "Uncle Jack" Bowden, a career Boy Scout, once told me, "Never let the truth stand in the way of a good story." Works for me! It has been good advise.

What's a book, even a cookbook, without a few stories? Some of these stories are true. I am certain of it. Some, I am equally certain, have been embellished. Some are out right made up. Some are borrowed, with permission. Some are stolen, but we tried to steal from the best.

Some, I hope, will make you laugh. Some may make you cry. Some may make you think. Whatever effect these little homilies have on you, the reader, I hope you enjoy them. And as far as I'm concerned, you may feel free to share them with others and tell them for your own.

Again I say, enjoy!

No Spot Is So Dear

"There's a church in the valley by the wildwood,
No lovelier spot in the dale;
No place is so dear to my childhood,
As the little brown church in the vale."

That song is by Dr. William Pitts. I used to sing it from the old Cokesbury Hymnal. You remember. The one with the brown cover. I always thought about my church as I sang that song, even though the Julia A. Porter United Methodist Church was not brown, but of red brick and was on a hill instead of in a vale. Of course, when I first started singing that song I didn't know what a vale was.

This weekend I needed to have my picture made for a book I've written that will be released, finally, in a few weeks. It's publication is only two years late, but that's another story. I decided to have the picture made in front of the Methodist Church in Porterdale.

One might think that having a picture made for a book cover is quite a complex process. I suppose that for some it is, but not for me. I put film in the camera, hand it to my wife Lisa, and ask her to take my picture. We had a grand old time Sunday afternoon in front of my childhood church. Our photo shoot probably lasted ten or fifteen minutes. We would have finished much sooner but after I had posed for 15 or 20 shots, Lisa realized there was no film in the camera. Once we overcame that obstacle, the wind refused to cooperate. Every time Lisa got ready to snap a picture the wind would begin to blow what little bit of hair I have left in every direction. We finally got what we hope will be a suitable shot.

We were about to get in our car and leave when I realized that I had not been inside the church in close to twenty years. How could that be? Where does the time go? We decided to go in, but the doors were locked. Hoping I wasn't being a bother, I knocked on the door of the parsonage, which is right beside the church. A gentleman wearing a white dress shirt and tie answered

151

the door. I knew I had the preacher. Nobody else in Porterdale would have on a white shirt and tie at three in the afternoon.

He was very gracious and volunteered to let us in the church before I even asked. He seemed genuinely glad to do it, too. Reverend Davis, which I learned was his name, escorted us around to the side door of the church, the one I was carried through when I was just a few days old to be placed on the Cradle Roll, as the list of Methodist babies was called in Porterdale.

The first thing I spotted was the water fountain. Surely it couldn't have been the same one my daddy held me up to when I was a toddler. I couldn't resist having a drink. The water tasted just the same, cold and pure.

As we walked into the sanctuary I felt at home. Time had gone backward. I looked up at the beautiful vaulted veiling and remembered all the times when I, as a boy, had tried, unsuccessfully, to count the boards that line the ceiling. I took in the beauty of the arched windows, with the sun shining through the frosted glass. I admired the glorious stained glass window behind the balcony. I sat in one of the pews for a moment.

To my wife, and children, and Reverend Davis, the church was empty. But not to me. All around me, on the seemingly empty pews, were the folk I grew up amongst. I could see each one, in their special places.

Marion Johnson was playing the organ. Neil Wheeler was leading the singing. Mrs. Annie Lee Day was in her spot in the choir loft and Red Few was in his. Someone once said that we always had a large and enthusiastic choir at Porterdale. Mrs. Annie was large and Red was enthusiastic.

Mrs. Estelle Allen was right down near the front, on the right side of the church. She may have been the sweetest woman I ever knew. I don't think she ever missed a funeral at our church. I could see Spunk Ivey and his wife Dora in my mind's eye, too. Mr. Ivey was Mayor of Porterdale forever and went over fifty years without missing a Sunday at church. Mrs. Ivey taught me Sunday School and prayed openly that I would make a preacher. I guess she'd be disappointed at how I turned out.

There were so many special people whose presence I felt in that empty church. They were mill people, for the most part, simple and honest and hard working. They came to church and gave their offerings and gave their time, lots of it, to children like me. They helped teach us right from wrong. They taught us important lessons like to turn to the middle of the Bible to find the Psalms, and to close our eyes when we prayed, and that we really needed to pay attention to the red words because they were the ones Jesus spoke. More importantly, they taught us that we were somebody and that we were loved.

I didn't want to take up too much of the preacher's afternoon, so we left before I was really ready to go. As we were leaving, though, I could make out the hymn that the angel choir was singing in my mind. It was "Precious Memories." How they linger. How they do linger.

Darrell Huckaby

"Peter asked, 'Lord, why do you speak to us in parables?' The Lord answered, 'Who then is the faithful and wise manager, whom the master puts in charge of his servants to give them their food allowance at the proper time? It will be good for the servant whom the master finds doing so when he returns. I tell you the truth, he will put him in charge of all his possessions. . .
. . . From everyone who has been given much, much will be demanded; and from those who have been entrusted with much, much more will be asked.'"

Luke 12: 41-43, 48

153

I Could Almost See the Scars

It was July hot in August. I don't know exactly what that means, but I heard it in a song once and liked the way it sounded. Taking my wife and three small children to Washington D.C. for summer vacation sounded like a good idea when we planned the trip—in February. After five days in our nation's capitol, we had had about all the fun we could stand for one week. It was the last morning of our trip and we were eating breakfast in the Union Station Food Court.

If you haven't been to Washington, you should. It's a national treasure. Sadly, it is overrun with homeless people, con artists, and panhandlers. Sometimes it is hard to tell them apart. During our week in Washington we had heard every conceivable story known to man in an effort to pry money away from the tourists. I had become very adept at ignoring pleading eyes and outstretched hands.

Back to Union Station. My wife had secured a table amidst the throng of people. I was trying to juggle two trays laden with biscuits, eggs, hash browns, coffee, orange juice, and the like—typical fast food breakfast fare. A young man in a green fatigue jacket came up to me. He had long hair, a three day old beard, and carried a backpack. I made a point not to look into his eyes as he approached me and asked for a handout. I didn't even pay attention to his words. I just gave him the brush off and began to sort out my family's food items.

The young man then did a strange thing. He thanked me, even though I hadn't given him anything, including one moment's attention.

I watched him as he walked up to a well dressed man at the next table. This was obviously a businessman, on his way to work. He was dressed in an expensive looking blue suit, a briefcase was at his feet, and he was reading the paper. This time I did listen to the young man, even though he wasn't talking to me. "Might I have a bit of breakfast?" he asked the fellow at the neighboring table.

The man looked up from his paper into the youngsters dark brown eyes. Without saying a word, the businessman tore in half the Styrofoam plate that held his breakfast and raked half of it onto the portion of the tray he had torn off. He handed this to the young beggar, along with an unopened carton of milk.

The young man thanked his benefactor, carried his breakfast over to a counter, then bowed his head and said grace before he began to eat.

I felt like two cents as those words from Matthew that I learned as a child and have taught my children echoed in my brain. "That which you do for the least of my kingdom, you also do to me."

I watched the stranger with new eyes as he picked up his food and began to eat. I could almost see the nail scars in the young man's hand.

Darrell Huckaby

"Then the righteous will answer him, 'Lord, when did we see you hungry and feed you, or thirsty and give you something to drink? When did we see you a stranger and invite you in, or needing clothes and clothe you? When did we see you sick or in prison and go to visit you?'
The King will reply, 'I tell you the truth, whatever you did for one of the least of these brothers of mine, you did for me.'"

Matthew 25: 37-4

BY GRACE ARE YOU SAVED

This is not original. I wish it were. I stole it from Mr. Moby, the morning disc jockey on WKHX Radio in Atlanta. I know he stole it from somebody else, so I don't mind using it in this book. Besides, it's for a good cause.

Seems a guy died and went to heaven. St. Peter, of course, met him at the Pearly Gates. The man asked what he had to do for admittance. St. Peter informed him that he had to score 100 points on a life survey.

"Fair enough," replied the man. "Fire away."

"Tell me about your family life," said St. Peter.

"I had a wonderful family," replied the man. "I was married to the love of my life for 65 years. I was never unfaithful to her, not even in my heart. We raised three wonderful kids who are all professionals with jobs and families of their own."

"Very good," responded St. Peter. "That's worth five points."

The man was a bit dismayed at the low score, but said nothing.

"I assume you are a church member," St, Peter continued. "Tell me about your work in your church."

The man's eyes brightened. "I have been a member of the same church for 86 years. I was baptized when I was six weeks old and confirmed into the church when I was twelve. I was president of the MYF and later taught youth and adult Sunday school classes. I have been Sunday school superintendent, Lay Leader, Chairmen of the Administrative Board and was in charge of the church barbecue for twenty years."

"Great," said St. Peter. "That's worth two more points. Only 93 to go."

The man looked a bit dismayed that his good church stewardship only earned him two points, but still he said nothing.

"Tell me about your community service," said St. Peter.

"Well," said the man, "I've been a member of the Lion's Club, the Rotary Club, and the Kiwanis. I served as Scoutmaster for thirty years. I was active in the Salvation Army, organized a food bank, worked one night a week at the homeless shelter and another night at a hospice."

"Those are all great works," commented St. Peter, "That's worth two points."

"Two points!" exclaimed the man. "At this rate it will be only by the Grace of God that I get in this place!"

"Bingo!" said, St. Peter. "Get a harp ready, boys, We've got another one!"

"But God shows his great love for us in this way; Christ died for us while we were still sinners."

Romans 5: 8

Bishop Pierce Harris and the Quarterly Conference

When he was pastor of the First Methodist Church of Atlanta, Pierce Harris often told a story on himself about a time when he was pastor of the Chickamauga Circuit, in north Georgia.

He and his wife awakened one cold winter's morning to discover that a thick blanket of snow lay over the entire Chickamauga Valley. The unfortunate thing about this unexpected snowstorm was that it had occurred on the eve of "Quarterly Conference Sunday." This was actually more than unfortunate. It was downright distressing, because in those days churches on a particular circuit would meet together at the conference and bring their "quarterledge," to the conference with them—three months worth of offering. It was from this offering that the pastor would receive his salary for that quarter.

Because of the rare snow storm, folks stayed away in droves and the offering was as meager as the attendance. Pierce said that he divided the funds with the Presiding Elder. Both were considerably short of the amount due them. He recounted that the worst part of all was the fact that he would have to tell his grocer, a deacon at the Baptist church, that he would have to make only a token payment on his grocery bill and carry the rest until the next payday.

When Reverend Harris and his young bride returned to the parsonage, Mary was crying and almost inconsolable. "Pierce," she asked through her tears, "What are we going to do?"

"Mary," he replied, "Put on your best dress. We are going into Chattanooga for dinner."

They went to the best restaurant in town and treated themselves to a scrumptious meal. Pierce paid the bill and left, in his words, "a right generous tip." When they walked out onto the sidewalk Pierce noticed a tobacco shop on the street corner. They went in and he bought a cigar with his last fifty cents.

On the way home, Mary again began to cry and lamented, "Pierce, what are we going to do for money?"

He replied in his gravelly voice, "Mary, for the next three months there won't be a dinner bell to ring in Chickamauga Valley that's out of our ear shot."

Reverend Harris would always end the story by adding, "If you were to go to the Chicamauga Valley today, people would tell you that Brother Pierce Harris was the visiting pastor to ever serve that charge."

Reverend David Hancock, Oak Grove UMC

"So the Twelve gathered all the disciples together and said, 'It would not be right for us to neglect the ministry of the word of God in order to wait on tables. Brothers, choose seven men from among you who are known to be full of the Spirit and wisdom. We will turn this responsibility over to them and will give our attention to prayer and the ministry of the word.'"

Acts 6: 2-4

Authors note: As a long time friend of David Hancock, I can attest to the fact that he took this passage of scripture to heart at every church gathering in which he was in attendance.

Jack Rawls Chile

There was a wonderful man in the Porterdale of my youth named Mr. Jack Rawls. Mr. Jack was a big man with half an ear on one side of his face. He was a friend to everyone he met, especially children, and a wonderful cook. He used to accompany our Boy Scout Troop to summer camp in the north Georgia mountains and cook for the whole group. If I live to be a hundred, I'll never forget the taste of Mr. Jack Rawls's fried chicken. He did wonderful things with fresh bream, too, and his pancakes took the pain out of getting up on a chilly mountain morning.

Mr. Jack Rawls also did a lot of cooking at our church. I'll never the Monday night he volunteered to cook chili for the United Methodist Men. He refused to allow anybody else in the kitchen with him. I guess Mr. Jack figured that if too many cooks spoiled the broth, they would do the same thing to chili. We all arrived at the meeting hungry and the delightful aroma drifting from the church kitchen into the fellowship hall was making all of our mouths water.

Finally, Mr. Jack declared the chili ready. Only then were two people allowed to enter the kitchen and bring the giant kettle of chili into the fellowship hall. We eagerly lined up to have our bowls filled with the rich and meaty concoction Mr. Jack had prepared for us. We filled our bowls to the brim and took our places along either side of the long table that stretched down the center of the room.

When grace had been said, as a man, we all took our long awaited first bite of the delectable chili. It was hotter than a twelve alarm fire. As soon as I swallowed the first bite my throat turned to fire and beads of sweat broke out on my forehead. I reached immediately for my iced tea glass. So did every other man at the table, except one.

All of us looked at one another. Everyone was gulping down tea as fast as we could. Sweat was pouring down our faces. At the same instant, everyone's eyes turned to the end of the table where Mr. Jack Rawls was seated, oblivious to the commotion his chili had caused. There he sat, with his pocket knife in his hand, cutting up hot red peppers into his bowl of chili.

Honesty compels me to admit that this is not Mr. Jack's original recipe. I got him to show me how to make chili after that memorable night, but I have, indeed, altered the recipe to protect the taste buds of those who might be brave enough to prepare this dish.

Mr. Jack's recipe fed a hundred people. I've scaled it down to serve eight and you can find it on page 54 of this book.

Darrell Huckaby

"Make a joyful noise unto the Lord, all ye lands.
Serve the Lord with gladness:
come before his presence with singing.
Know ye that the Lord he is God:
it is he that hath made us, and not we ourselves;
we are his people, and the sheep of his pasture.
Enter into his gates with thanksgiving
and into his courts with praise;
be thankful unto him, and bless his name.
For the Lord is good; his mercy is everlasting;
and his truth endureth to all generations."

Psalm 100

Barbecues, Bake Sales, and Such

Churches learned long ago that serving food to the general public was a good way to earn money beyond the tithes and offerings of the congregations. Barbecues and bake sales and such are not only excellent fund raisers, but also offer an opportunity for the fun and fellowship that goes so well with the preparation of large quantities of good food.

Church barbecues have long been annual affairs at many churches across the South. In fact, my church, Ebenezer UMC in Conyers, has a traditional barbecue, with pulled pork, Brunswick stew and cole slaw every spring and a chicken barbecue in the fall. Everyone with an ounce of Southern blood knows that barbecue has to be cooked slow over hot coals and basted with secret formula sauces. There is as much disagreement over what goes into Brunswick stew as there is over infant baptism. My Brunswick stew recipe can be found on page 33.

Most churches have bake sales in conjunction with other events, but some have them in and of themselves. I have to admit though, I've seen more and more store bought cakes and pies at church sales lately and fewer and fewer home made desserts. It's a sign of the times, I suppose.

Some churches find other creative ways to raise funds through church dinners. One church I know turns their fellowship hall into a romantic Italian restaurant every Valentine's Day. They have red checkered table cloths, candle light, soft music, and spaghetti. It's the hit of the season. The husbands get off the hook relatively cheap and the church missions fund is greatly enriched.

Pancake breakfasts seem to be popular, too, especially during the holiday shopping season. The men of most churches seem to take great pride in being able to prepare breakfast. Hotcakes and sausage with warm maple syrup would put anybody in a happy frame of mind. I guess that's why they're so often held during the shopping season. The women not only get the men to cook, but also put them in a great frame of mind.

They happily send their wives shopping while they stay behind to clean up the church. What a racket!

Church dinners as fund raisers are universal. I visited a church in England that raised money for a new organ by sponsoring a wine tasting. You won't hear of that happening in South Georgia.

I took a group to Hawaii once and a church family prepared a luau for us as a way to earn funds. The food was surpassed only by the hospitality of the island people.

In parts of Maine, lobster dinners can be purchased in church basements and one can find church sponsored fish fries all across our great country.

One of the most unusual traditions concerning church dinners that I know anything about are the oyster suppers that are held at the Walnut Grove United Methodist Church every autumn. Walnut Grove is a small community in Walton County, Georgia. People used to come from far and wide to eat delectable fried oysters, always the largest available, cole slaw, and oyster stew.

My aunt, Agnes Thompson, affectionately known by us as Aunt Snow, was a member of the church and rolled oysters for church dinners for decades. The oysters were so delicious because of the special way they were rolled in bread crumbs and because of the special batter used to prepare them. I tried to get a recipe for those fried oysters to be included in this book. I would have had more success getting the Coca Cola formula or the combination to the vault at Ft. Knox.

I have many fond memories of those oyster dinners. Because of them, I learned to enjoy eating oysters as a small boy. Having learned to eat oysters, I realized that I could eat almost anything. Two incidents that occurred at Walnut Grove particularly stand out in my mind.

There was, and still is, beside the church at Walnut Grove, and old iron bell tower. As a very young boy I used to visit the church with my aunt and uncle and was sometimes allowed to ring the bell to signal the time for Sunday school to begin, the bell chord lifting me high into the air.

I was with my parents at an oyster supper, waiting for dinner to be served. Dozens of people were waiting around, wanting to get the first batch of oysters as they came out of the pans. One of the church members emerged from the basement fellowship hall to signal that the first seating was about to begin. He grabbed the bell chord and gave it several hard pulls. The problem was, this was the first oyster supper of the season and, apparently, the first time the bell had been rung in a while.

The biggest wasp nest in the history of the world had been built in the old bell during the summer and was still active. The wasps didn't appreciate being disturbed one bit. What seemed like hundreds of the creatures swarmed down among the people. I've never seen so many men, women, and children move so quickly in so many different directions.

I visited the Walnut Grove church recently. I noticed that the old bell is still there, but no rope is attached.

Another incident that I remember, more from my daddy's telling than my own memory, involved sugar dishes. It seems that the girls of the church who were given the responsibility of setting the tables for the oyster suppers filled the sugar dishes with salt instead of sugar. I'm pretty sure my cousin, Carolyn, was one of the girls involved. They all claimed it was an honest mistake. Knowing my cousin as I do, I tend to doubt that.

My daddy never tired of telling how he put two heaping teaspoons of what he thought was sugar into his coffee, stirring it, and then taking a sip. I'm pretty sure he spit it right back into the cup, even though he was out in public.

I know that my cousin's prank had a lasting impact on him because for the rest of his days, whenever he encountered a sugar dish in a public place he would put a tiny amount on his finger and taste it to make sure it wasn't salt.

I'll say again—Precious memories. How they do linger.

Darrell Huckaby

Seven Step Johnny Cake

There has been much discussion about how today's generation doesn't seem to cook as many home made desserts as previous generations. This "recipe" for "Johnny Cake" might explain why that is.

1. Light oven; get out utensils and ingredients. Remove blocks, trucks, cars, and other assorted toys from table. Grease pan and crack nuts.
2. Measure 2 cups of flour; Remove Johnny's hands from flour; wash flour off him. Remeasure flour.
3. Put flour, baking powder and salt in sifter. Get dust pan and brush up pieces of the bowl Johnny knocked onto the floor. Get another bowl. Answer the doorbell.
4. Return to kitchen. Remove Johnny's hand from bowl. Wash Johnny. Answer the phone. Return to kitchen. Remove quarter inch of salt from greased pan. Look for Johnny. Grease another pan. Answer the phone.
5. Return to kitchen. Remove Johnny's hand from bowl. Take up greased pan and find layer of nutshells in it. Look for Johnny, who ran after knocking bowl off the table again. Wash the table, walls, and dishes. Mop the floor.
6. Call the bakery and order a cake.

7. Take two aspirin and lie down.

Peg Rosing

165

We Steal From the Best

This came to us from Vicki H. Smith, who at the time of the submission was Associate Pastor at Cannon United Methodist in Snellville. Reverend Smith asked her congregation to complete the sentence, "You might be a Methodist if..." She was doing a little takeoff, you see, on Jeff Foxworthy's "You might be a redneck..." By her own admission, Rev. Smith borrowed/stole the idea from Mulkey West who got the idea from Crede Hinshaw at Mulberry Street UMC in Macon, who got the idea from Dr. John Page, Senior Pastor of Marvin UMC in Martinez.

She particularly liked the response of Betty Hodges, widow of the late Rev. Jud Hodges, a long time Methodist minister.

You might be a Methodist if...

You think the keys to the kingdom are shaped like a knife and fork.

We decided that as long as there was so much stealing going on that in addition to the item Rev. Smith sent us, we would print some others from her church newsletter. Reverend Smith and the congregation at Cannon UMC should take heart in knowing that while we have stolen for this publication, we have only stolen from the best.

You might be a Methodist if . . .

. . . you have ever referred to baptism by immersion as "slam dunking."

. . . you will sit through a hurricane to watch a college football game but stay home from church when it looks like rain.

. . . you have ever been personally responsible for a restaurant discontinuing fried chicken as an all you can eat item on its menu.

. . . you have ever asked for "seconds" at communion.

. . . you have ever referred to a church barbecue as a religious experience.

. . . you have a deep seated conviction that entrance to heaven will require a covered dish.

. . . you think Jesus chose twelve disciples because everyone knows that all good works are done through committees.

The last item reminds me of something Bishop Arthur Moore is reported to have said. "I am firmly convinced that the Methodist Church is so well organized that it will endure long after Christianity has vanished from the earth."

Let the Women Lead the Way

Do you know what would have happened if it had been Three Wise Women instead of Three Wise Men?

They would have asked for directions, arrived on time, helped deliver the baby, cleaned the stable, made a casserole, and brought practical gifts.

Lorraine Simpson, Garden City

167

Homecoming in May

When I was a child in Thomasville, the church we belonged to had Homecoming on the first Sunday in May each year. After morning service, the side street was blocked off, tables set up, and families spread baskets of home-cooked food to enjoy dinner together.

On one such day, a couple came up rolling a baby carriage. They were not members of the church, but, nonetheless, proceeded to lift cakes, pies, meats, and every other dish imaginable from the table. They loaded it all into the carriage, which we discovered held no baby.

Some of the people told the preacher and wanted to go after them, but he said, "No. They might be hungry and we have plenty of good food left to eat."

That homecoming, so many years ago, was the first time I ever looked at a situation and stopped to think what Jesus might have done. I believe he would have done the same as our preacher.

Nell R. Brannon, Carrollton

Judging a Pie by the Pie Pan

If you ever have the opportunity to attend an old time church dinner and can't choose from all the goodies on the dessert table—always look for the pie in the old blackened tin pan. It will be good because the person that brought it has had years and years of experience at baking pies.

I've used this technique for many, many years and have never had a bad piece of pie yet.

Joan Brandenburg, Concord

Childhood Memory

When I was a child, people usually brought their many dishes to "dinner on the grounds" in large cardboard boxes. After the dishes were placed on the table, the boxes were placed upside down beneath the table and the small children used these as their tables. I suppose, since the "box tables" were well hidden by the table clothes, I thought I could get away with eating all the butterscotch pie I wanted. Needless to say, I did not feel well for the rest of the day and I have not eaten butterscotch pie since that day.

Emily R. Barwick, Sandy Cross UMC, Crawfordsville

A Simple Grace

A friend of mine who had never prayed aloud, not even to offer a simple table grace, was called upon unexpectedly to bless the food at a family meal. With all heads bowed he offered this simple and truthful invocation:

"Thank you, Lord, for this food. If I hadn't of worked fer it I wouldn't of had it.

Amen!

Earline R. Cole, Bonaire UMC

". . . I am the bread of life;
he who comes to me shall not hunger,
and he who believes in me shall never thirst."

John 6: 35

169

Camp Meeting Meals Are Unsurpassed

One recent summer I was afforded the opportunity of preaching at Lumpkin Campground in Dawson County, Georgia. One of the by-products of this experience was the fact that I began my ministry in Lumpkin/Dawson County some 33 years earlier. As a young and inexperienced pastor, I found one of the most memorable remembrances of those early days was the way the churches kept their pastors fed. Never a Sunday passed when I did not receive an invitation to the home of one of my parishioners for a delicious Sunday dinner.

Being from the North, some of the cultural differences became very apparent. The one that remains clearest in my mind is the fact that the men, in those days, would always eat first. After the men had finished, the women would eat, and then the children. (This tradition is no longer practiced.)

The folks at Lumpkin reminded me again of how good the people in that area cook. Three large meals a day kept me stuffed, but, somehow, anticipating the next meal.

At my last service of preaching, I told the people that they might want to consider inviting one preacher to preach and another just to eat! The food was great, and I found my spirit and body filled to overflowing.

Philip D. DeMore, First UMC, Gainesville

**"And you shall know the truth,
and the truth shall make you free."**

John 8: 32

A Dinner on the Grounds Tale

When he came to church on Sundays, he came walking. His attendance at worship was sporadic, at best. But he never missed a Sunday when there was to be dinner served on the church grounds. On those Sundays he would arrive at church pulling a little red wagon, the kind children used to coast in, down hills. After everyone had finished their indulgent meals, the man could be seen leaving the church premises, pulling his little red wagon. The man may have shown up with his wagon empty, but upon returning home he made sure it was filled with a bountiful supply of leftover food.

Bishop C. W. "Handy" Hancock, Retired—South Georgia Conference

". . . Jesus said to Simon Peter, 'Simon, son of John, do you truly love me more than these?'
'Yes, Lord,' he said, 'you know that I love you.'
Jesus said, 'Feed my lambs.'
Again Jesus said, 'Simon, son of John, do you truly love me?'
He answered, 'Yes, Lord, you know that I love you.'
Jesus said, 'Take care of my sheep.'
The third time he said to him, 'Simon, son of John, do you love me?'
Peter was hurt because Jesus asked him the third time, 'Do you love me?'
He said, 'Lord, you know all things; you know that I love you.'
Jesus said, 'Feed my sheep.'

John 21: 15-17

A Young Boy Learns a Lesson

I was seventeen, a mill boy from Porterdale. My parents, although they could not afford it, wanted to host a dinner for my basketball team—the Newton County Rams. High school basketball was big in Newton County. Some people said that we played school and taught basketball. That wasn't really the case, but the basketball team was revered in that county in the '60's. Local businessmen often treated us to dinners and trips, so having a team feed was not unusual. Having it hosted by my family was.

The dinner was to be a barbecue, held in the cafeteria of the Porterdale School. I was pleased that my family was going to actually host the team and looked forward to the night for weeks. That is, until I learned that my daddy intended to get up and speak to the team. If that wasn't bad enough, my mother had asked a friend from work, Iris Standard, to invite her preacher to deliver a message.

I was mortified. We couldn't just show up and eat like we usually did at these functions. We had to listen to my daddy make a speech and sit through a talk by a preacher! And it was all my fault.

When the night of the dinner arrived I was in a self induced blue funk. I sat in misery, barely able to eat the barbecue, stew, and coleslaw, even though it was delicious. I was too worried that my father would embarrass me in his remarks and that the preacher would talk forever. To my surprise, my father kept his remarks short and did a great job. He was funny and even eloquent in his praise of our team and our efforts. I began to feel a little ashamed that I ever thought he would embarrass me.

Then my mother introduced the preacher. He was very slight in stature, had a high pitched voice and wore thick eyeglasses. He looked a little out of place in the room full of athletes. His name was Phil DeMore.

He got our attention right away by telling a bogus story about the legendary Alabama football coach, Bear Bryant. He had us stand up and do a reaction drill that Coach Bryant supposedly did with his team. He stood in front of the room, his arms widespread and his hands clinched into two fists. Reverend DeMore would slowly bring his arms toward one another, sometimes crossing one over the other, sometimes stopping just short of doing so. The preacher had instructed us to clap our hands, once, very sharply, every time one of his hands crossed over the other. He started very slowly and deliberately and tried to trick us into clapping out of turn.

Once we got the hang of the drill he began moving his hands faster and faster. Pretty soon we were all clapping wildly. He had started his speech by tricking us into giving him a standing ovation.

From that point on, he owned us. He kept us in stitches for half an hour and then left us with a great message, with which we could all identify, about commitment and paying the price.

I went a long way toward growing up that night. I was never again embarrassed by my parents in any way. I learned to trust their judgment and became one of Reverend Philip DeMore's biggest fans.

By the way, I've used his little trick to begin hundreds of speeches myself.

Darrell Huckaby

173

High Water

My daddy used to tell this story about a little country church in the low lands of South Georgia, down near the pine barrens. The church was going to have homecoming for the first time in several years and old man Gus, who was sort of the patriarch of the little congregation, wanted everything to be just right for the big day. Gus took great pride in the church grounds and he planned to have them looking better than they ever had for this special homecoming.

As luck would have it, a rainy spell set in about two weeks before the big day. It rained several inches every day for over a week. Needless to say, Gus didn't get any yard work done, and he became more and more irritable and more and more determined to put the grounds in order.

Two days before the big event, Gus's luck changed—for the worse. The steady rain turned into a deluge. It wasn't as bad as Noah's flood, but close to it, or so it seemed to Gus.

On the Saturday before Homecoming Sunday the water had risen to flood levels. In fact, it was the worse flood with the highest water people in those parts had ever seen. The ladies of the church, realizing that there would be no dinner on the grounds that year, met on Saturday morning to put the small fellowship hall in order . The were determined that Homecoming would not be rained out.

As they were sitting around a table, folding napkins and silverware into little bundles they noticed a curious sight—a yellow hat floated by on the floodwaters outside the windows of the fellowship hall. A few minutes later it floated by in the opposite direction. The women began to watch the hat and noticed that the hat was floating back and forth from one side of the flooded church yard to the other, in a symmetrical pattern.

They were standing at the window, staring at the yellow hat in amazement, when Lucille, the church dowager, came into the room. "What in the world are you all staring at?" she demanded.

The women showed her the floating yellow hat. "Oh, that," she responded. "That's just Gus. He told me last night that come hell or high water he was going to cut the grass today so the yard would look good for Homecoming."

Darrell Huckaby

*"Therefore I urge you, brothers, in view of God's mercy,
to offer your bodies as living sacrifices,
holy and pleasing to God--this is your
spiritual act of worship.
Do not conform any longer to the pattern of this world,
but be transformed by the renewing of your mind.
Then you will be able to test and approve what God's will is;
his good, pleasing and perfect will."*

Romans 12: 1-2

Blind Faith

Gus may very well be the same old guy in the story told by the late Lewis Grizzard, and many others. Seems a flood had come to a small town, perhaps the same town in the previous story, and the authorities had ordered an evacuation of the low lying areas near the river.

Every person in the valley left except one ornery old man, probably Gus.

Water had reached the bottom of his porch and the local sheriff came by in a row boat to rescue him. "Get in the boat, Gus," pleaded the constable. "The water's going to get higher."

"I'm staying right here," proclaimed Gus. "The Lord's going to take care of me."

The rain continued to fall and the water continued to rise. Gus had to climb out a second story window and seek safety on the roof. The Civil Defense sent a motor boat to save him. The water was up to the eaves of his house.

"Get in the boat, Gus," pleaded the CD director. "The water's going to get higher."

"I'm staying right here," answered the stubborn old man. "The Lord's going to take care of me,"

The rain continued to fall and the water continued to rise. Gus had to climb to the top of his chimney. He was clinging for dear life when a helicopter from the state government flew over. The governor himself was in the helicopter. He shouted down through a bull horn. "Climb up the ladder Gus. The water's going to get higher. Your house will float away."

"I'm staying right here," Gus insisted. "The Lord's going to take care of me."

Seeing that the old man couldn't be swayed, the governor and the helicopter finally flew away. The rain continued, the water rose, and Gus drowned.

When he got to heaven and came face to face with St. Peter, he demanded to see the Lord, right away. St. Peter granted him his wish.

Gus chastised the Lord. "God," he said, "I believed in you. I had faith in you. I thought you would save me. Why did you let me drown?"

"For goodness sakes, Gus," replied the Lord. "I sent two boats and a helicopter. What else did you want?"

Darrell Huckaby

". . . the fruit of the Spirit is
love, joy, peace,
patience, kindness,
goodness, faithfulness,
gentleness, self-control;
against such things there is no law."

Galatians 5: 22-23

177

Preachin' or Meddlin'?

When I was an undergraduate student at the University of Georgia I was invited, by a young lady friend, to homecoming at her little country church. There was to be a normal church service, dinner, of course, on the grounds, and then a Gospel singing afterward.

We got there just as the service started and had to look hard to find a seat as the little white frame building was filled to capacity. I found myself sitting on the second pew beside a rail thin lady who appeared to be at least ninety years old.

The homecoming speaker was a young man from the congregation who had answered the call to preach and was just finishing his seminary work. The young preacher, obviously eager to show the home folks what he had learned, preached an hour long sermon that was full of fire and brimstone. I believe he touched on every sin with which I was even vaguely familiar.

The lady sitting beside me was a very active worshiper. The preacher spoke out against the evils of alcohol, extorting the congregation to give up wine, beer, and moonshine whiskey.

The lady beside me shouted, "Amen!" several times, and dug her rather sharp elbow into my side. "That young man's doing some real preaching!" she exclaimed.

Then the preacher talked about the sin of gambling. He compared Las Vegas with Sodom and Gomorrah and urged people to stand up against the evils of poker, pin ball machine payouts, and pulling numbers on a punch board.

"Amen," shouted the lady beside me as she continued to dig her elbow into my now tender side. "That young man is doing some powerful preaching!"

178

Next the preacher attacked lust, speaking out against pornographic magazines and those who attended the hoochy koochy show at the county fair.

"Amen! Amen! Double Amen!" shouted my pew mate. She almost cracked my ribs with her elbow. "That fine young man is doing some of the best preaching I've ever heard!" she said to me.

Then the young man turned his tirade against the evil weed, tobacco. He reminded those present that our body was a temple of God and that we shouldn't destroy it by smoking cigarettes and pipes and, heaven forbid, by dipping snuff!

The lady beside me stood up abruptly. She tapped my leg with her cane and demanded, "Let me by!":

"But ma'am," I asked, "Where are you going?"

"I'm going to help the other ladies prepare the dinner," she replied. "That young whippersnapper has done quit preachin' and gone to meddlin'!"

Darrell Huckaby

". . . Love the Lord your God with all your heart,
all your soul, and all your mind.
This is the first and most important command.
And the second command is like the first:
Love your neighbor as you love yourself."

Matthew 22: 37-39

179

Train Up a Child in the Ways of the Lord

My first spiritual leader was my father, Homer Huckaby. That's the way it should be. The Bible teaches us that if we train up a child in the ways of the Lord, when he grows older he will not stray.

My daddy and my church were and are synonymous in my mind. Homer Huckaby worked hard in a cotton mill six days a week. He worked the second shift, which meant that he was gone to work when I came home from school and that I was in bed when he came home from work. On Saturdays, he worked the day shift. I missed spending time with him.

But on Sunday mornings, he took me to church. I can still remember the hustle and bustle of getting ready for church on Sunday morning. He set a good example for me. He taught me about the Bible and about the grace of God. For years he taught an adult Sunday school class and I would rush from my own class as soon as the teacher dismissed us so that I could slide in the back door of his class room and listen to him discuss the Bible.

My daddy was not a saint, nor did he pretend to be. But he was saved by the Grace of Jesus Christ. For that I am eternally grateful. For years and years he kept a Bible verse taped to his shaving mirror. It reminded him of a truth that has served me well through the ups and downs of my life. It read:

> *"And we know that all things work together for good*
> *to them that love God,*
> *to them who are called according to his purpose."*
> *Romans 8: 28*

Life has taught me to say a big "amen" to that, and a big thanks to my father who taught me so much about the Lord's goodness and his grace.

A Little Child Shall Lead Them

I wish I could say that I remember this event. Well, I could say that I do, but it wouldn't be the truth. While that has never stopped me before, this time I'll just admit that I don't remember the incident but have been told the story so many times by so many people that I'm sure it must have happened.

I was just a toddler and could barely talk, but had learned to offer my own brand of grace before meals at home. I was too young, even, for "God is great, God is good..." None the less, when my daddy would call for a blessing at supper time I would reverently fold my hands, bow my head, and say, "Ask the blessing, ask the blessing, ask the blessing. Amen."

We were welcoming a new preacher to the Porterdale Methodist Church with a covered dish dinner in the church fellowship hall. My father had the honor of introducing the preacher. When he did, he asked the preacher, Preacher Peters, I believe it was, to bless the meal.

That was my cue. I stepped forward, bowed my head, and in a loud voice said, "Ask the blessing, ask the blessing, ask the blessing. Amen."

Everyone laughed, of course. My father then said, "Preacher Peters, would you return thanks."

Again, I took that as my cue, stepped forward and said the same thing, this time even louder as I assumed my daddy had not heard the first effort.

Preacher Peters, in his infinite wisdom, spoke up and said, "That grace is, indeed, sufficient for me. Let's eat!"

That remark instantly endeared the new preacher to our congregation, especially my mama and daddy.

Darrell Huckaby

WHAT WOULD JESUS DO?
REST WHEN HE WAS TIRED FOR ONE THING

"In the beginning was the Word, and the Word was with God, and the Word was God. . . And the Word became flesh and dwelt among us." I didn't write that. John did. A long time ago.

Pretty neat story, huh? What a concept. God came to earth and lived among the people. Not only did he live with us, he was one of us. The Bible tells us that while he was a man on earth Jesus was a man on earth. He lived with his family, ate food, drank wine, worked in his daddy's carpenter shop, went fishing with the boys, and did what people do. He knew temptation and fear, minded his mama, and even cried when his friend died.

He spent three years as an itinerate preacher. Did real well, too. It's been two thousand years and folks are still talking about his sermons. He walked all over his part of the world, never had a parsonage to call his own, cared for the sick, fed the hungry, and taught the people. Of course he had to attend numerous committee meetings with his disciples. With a schedule like that it stands to reason that Jesus, having become a man, would get tired. When he got tired, he withdrew from his work and rested. Says so right there in the Bible, in several places.

Jesus came to earth, of course, to die for our sins. I'm no theologian, but I also believe he came to show us how we should live our lives. Even Jesus rested when he was tired, and he knew that he couldn't really rest in the midst of all the hubbub and confusion he lived and worked in. Time after time scripture tells us Jesus went off alone to rest and pray, to commune with his Father.

Jesus was showing us what we should do. In today's world we move in dozens of directions at the same time. We work too much so that we can buy things and store up riches on earth. We drive our kids around at a dizzying pace, trying to keep them in every activity imaginable. The busier we are, the more we seem to take on. I'm more guilty than anybody. Sometimes we need to do what Jesus did when he got tired. We need to find a place of solitude. We need to rest. We need to talk to God. We need to listen for His reply.

My family and I did that over a recent weekend. We found a marvelous place called Covecrest Christian Retreat and Conference Center in the north Georgia mountains. We rented a little cabin. It had a kitchen and a front porch with rocking chairs, but didn't have a television or telephone or any other electronic devise. My kids didn't know how they would survive.

They survived by fishing in the pond, walking in the creek, climbing nearby mountains, and standing under an icy cold waterfall. We even sat on the front porch and read books and pulled out a dusty Cokesbury hymnal and sang camp meeting songs.

Jesus knew what he was doing when he went off alone to rest. We should try it more often. It makes life better. I wonder how many other good examples he set for us.

Darrell Huckaby

"God blessed the seventh day and made it a holy day, because on that day he rested from all the work he had done in creating the world."

Genesis 2: 3

Recipe Index

Dinner On the Grounds
Second Helping

If you missed out on the opportunity to contribute to this unique book, please send your favorite church stories and recipes to:

Darrell Huckaby
2755 Ebenezer Rd.
Conyers, GA 30094

There are many additional stories and recipes out there, just waiting to be published in another book. Thank you for your interest and support.

ADDITIONAL COPIES OF
DINNER ON THE GROUNDS

Fill Out the Form Below and Mail, Along With Your Check. Please include $15.00 per book and $3.00 postage and handling per order.

Please send me _____ copies of

Dinner on the Grounds.................$15.00 each_____

Postage and handling................ $3.00 each_____

TOTAL ENCLOSED $ _____

Name _____

Address _____

City _____ State _____ Zip _____

If you would like your book(s) autographed by the author, please indicate below. Please print the spelling of the person(s) names to whom you want the signature addressed.

Please autograph book to:

_____

Please make checks payable to:
Southland Press
1108 Monticello Street
Covington, GA 30014

www.darrellhuckaby.com

DOES YOUR CHURCH GROUP OR ORGANIZATION NEED A SPEAKER?

If your group is looking for an entertaining and inspirational speaker, contact Darrell Huckaby. He is a dynamic speaker, always funny, and can tailor his talk to fit any occasion. He particularly enjoys sharing his semi-funny stories laced with common-sense Gospel lessons with Southern congregations on Wednesday and Sunday evenings--or Sunday mornings if dinner is served on the grounds afterward! He can be contacted directly by phone at his home in Conyers, Georgia or through his website **www.darrellhuckaby.com**

Contact Darrell Huckaby today to assure the best meeting your group will have all year.

The Lord's Prayer

Our Father, who art in heaven,
Hallowed be thy name.
Thy Kingdom come, thy will be done,
on earth, as it is in heaven.
Give us this day our daily bread,
Forgive us our trespasses,
as we forgive those
that trespass against us.
Lead us not into temptation,
but deliver us from evil.
[For thine is the kingdom, and the
power, and the glory,
Forever.]
Amen

Luke 11: 4